I
Have
A
Reason

For Patty + Tom Moore

TULSA

Prov. 18:21

ISBN: 978-1-957262-55-0

I Have a Reason

This book is a memoir. It depicts the author's recollection of past experiences. Some details are based on interviews with past acquaintances. This book is mostly true, but some names and details have been changed to protect people's privacy. In some instances, the actions of multiple people were combined into one fictional character. Dialogue had to be recreated, so it is not perfectly factual. Not all events are written in chronological order. This book does not replace counseling by a mental health professional.

Yorkshire Publishing
1425 E 41st Pl
Tulsa, OK 74105
www.YorkshirePublishing.com
918.394.2665

Published in the USA

I
Have
A
Reason

An
Autistic
Perspective
On
Bullying

JOEY PERRY

CONTENTS

This book is dedicated to the man I'm told I sound like. Grandpa, you were never afraid to tell me the truth. You said it whether I wanted to hear it or not. When the truth stung, that's exactly when I needed it the most. The truth led me to become the man I am. For that, thanks.

CHAPTER ONE — Diagnosis

I had no way of knowing that I was abnormal. What kind of normal was there to compare myself to? None. I didn't grasp what everyone was so worried about. I had my own room, a bucket of Legos, and more home-cooked food than I could eat. That's all I needed to be happy at eight years old. I didn't know what autism was. I had never heard that word before. What happened outside of my bedroom door was none of my concern. I couldn't have cared less. Finishing the Lego castle was my only priority. Life was truly that simple.

I closed my door to drown out the noise so I could focus. Grandma was arguing with someone on the phone. Suddenly, her southern dialect came out. Clearly, things were getting heated. I rolled my eyes and mumbled, "Whatever it is, I didn't do it." I tiptoed to the kitchen so I could hear better. She yelled, "I know what I am talking about! I am certified in special education, and I am about to have a second master's degree. On top of that, my husband has a bachelor's in psychology. We are not dumb old hicks like you think we are! You can take that invoice and stick it where the sun doesn't shine! People are going to know about this, don't think they won't!"

She hung up and slammed the phone on the counter. A plate fell from the cupboard and shattered everywhere. I jumped backward. I heard Grandpa's cigarette cough as the front door slammed. "What the hell is going on in here?" Grandma tossed her dishrag in the sink and crossed her arms. I slipped into the hallway to remain anonymous. I put my ear to the wall and listened to the rest. She whispered, "You know what I think? I think Joey is autistic. I am not 100% sure, but I think he is. I am going to make an appointment with a psychologist this time. That lady doesn't have the brains God gave a dead goose. I'm never taking him there again."

Grandpa exclaimed with glee, "I've been telling you to do that for a while now! We'll never know for sure unless we take him to a real doc. It's about time!" She stormed off. "Well, now I am! Here's your coat. Let's go." "Uh...I can't, dear. I have to be at the yard by four to pick up that load." She tossed the coat and said, "Can't they get someone else to do it?" He exasperated. "That isn't how truck driving works! I warned you that things would be tight for a while." He put out the cigarette and walked out with a duffel bag over his shoulder.

I followed Grandpa out and waited for Grandma to follow. I stared at the endless countryside surrounding us. There were no neighbors as far as the eye could see. A pack of deer weaved through the meadow. They trotted past an old mailbox on the back fence. Supposedly, that used to be a road leading to an oil lease or cattle trail. The house was a hundred years old, so that could have just been a legend. It nearly predated the state of Oklahoma. It was anyone's guess whether the floors were creaking from someone walking, or just the wind. The decayed barn next door always gave me the creeps. A big dent in our garage came from the previous owner; he had gotten tipsy and backed a tractor into it. Honeysuckle wrapped around the chicken wire fences. It was so thick that I couldn't see the road down there. Grandpa fired up the Blazer and left for the truck stop.

We got in the Camry. The cattle guards clicked as we left the driveway. "Joey, we are going to see an expert." I banged on the window and yelled, "No, no, no! I'm not going! She is terrifying! I hate her!" Grandma chuckled a bit. "Relax, it is not that crazy witch we've been going to. You never have to see her again. This guy is a clinical psychologist. I have heard good things about him. Give it a chance; I think you'll like him." I still wasn't so sure. "I could be finishing my Lego set right now! This is a waste of time. What is a psychologist anyway?" She said, "if you do this for me and behave, I will take you to Long John Silver's." "Okay!" It was a mile to the highway and twenty more to the city.

We pulled up to a modern-looking complex. It was an angular building with a skylight in the lobby. The receptionist nodded for us to come on back. We took a seat in Dr. Mac's office. "So, we got my grandson Joey at one year old. He didn't start talking until he was four. He has a hard time connecting with people. He has to have things a specific way, and he can't handle loud noises. He is smarter than people think, though. I know he is because he can just...see things. He is very obsessive about everything he does. Intelligence isn't the problem here. Someone tried to diagnose him with PDDNOS, pervasive development disorder not otherwise specified. I think that man got it wrong. There is something different going on." Dr. Mac set his clipboard down and clicked his pen. He looked down at me and thought about it for a second. "Tell you what, I will schedule some tests next week."

It didn't take long for him to figure it out. He recognized what I had after a few sessions. He picked the clipboard up again and started writing fast. The official diagnosis was "Asperger Syndrome." He grabbed some brochures to dive in further. Take note that the terminology has changed since then. The clinical term was changed to "Level 1 ASD: Autism Spectrum Disorder" in the late 2000s.

Grandma's suspicions were confirmed. She grabbed her school ID badge and set it on the coffee table. "I work with kids who are on the spectrum every day. My husband has a bachelor's in psychology. A bunch of people acted like we were crazy. You wouldn't believe how little some people know. That last counselor was a raving lunatic! She thought she knew everything, but she didn't have a clue. She would hold him down, make him claustrophobic, and I couldn't take it anymore. If Joey knew we were going to her office, he screamed so loud that I got a migraine; I am not kidding you. If someone treated me like that, I'd lose my mind too! On top of all that, she had the audacity to ask me to pay for a canceled appointment! She can forget that...it's not happening! We're never going there again. I'm so glad I came here. I have heard nothing but good things from my friend that recommended you. I knew Joey was smarter than they thought he was. I just knew it. You don't have to dumb things down or sugarcoat them like other people have done. I want the truth. Now that we know he's autistic, what can we do for him?"

The doctor looked amused. "I got a sense that you had some background knowledge from what the receptionist told me. Joey is incredibly lucky to have you. So many parents get the wrong idea after hearing a diagnosis like this; they tend to get overwhelmed. You, on the other hand, understand what autism is and what it isn't. If you guys keep working with him like you are now, he can lead a productive life. I think he can accomplish whatever he sets his mind to. It will be a different road for him than most people, but that doesn't have to be a bad thing. He can do this."

He looked down at me, then back at her. He took a deep breath. "The social aspect is probably going to be his biggest struggle to overcome. Right now, the other kids aren't noticing that he is different than they are. It is obvious to adults like you and me, but not to them. His peers are way too young to see him that way yet. In their eyes, he is still just like them. In a few years, they will start noticing the differences. That gap will grow bigger, and that is when the troubles will start. It may become difficult for him to socialize at the same level as the other kids. Unfortunately, this often leads to misunderstandings and even bullying in some cases. Those early teenage years are what we should be concerned with. That is when he will need the most help. Having a place that he can go and ask questions or get support is a good start. You've already begun building that. I believe, with your support and good therapy, the gap will actually get smaller again. That is absolutely attainable. Let's keep in touch and check in every month or so. If something comes up, we can start doing more frequent appointments if needed. How does that sound?"

"Works for me."

As Grandma said, I was four years old when I started talking. This was definitely later than most children. I should have at least been saying simple words and even short sentences. That was not the case with me. Grandma could understand what some sounds I made meant. Grandpa could understand some of the others, but no one could fully crack the code. "heel-way" was the only decipherable sound before that time. Sometimes it meant I was ready to eat, and other times it just meant I was pointing at an oil drilling rig.

Speech therapy was not cheap. We went to a state agency office to get approved for aid. The lady at the agency did everything in her power to make it difficult. She initially claimed that she could understand me if she tried and that she had seen some of the most intensely autistic children in the state. She criticized my grandparents until she got me in a room alone. She could not understand one word I said. I might as well have been Chewbacca trying to talk to the empire. She threw her hands up and grabbed her notary stamp. We were approved in two shakes of a lamb's tail.

I started going to speech therapy every week. Having a consistent routine worked for me. My autism made me very uncomfortable with change. I needed a systematic routine to follow. Every week, I knew what to expect at the therapy session. We repeated various words and sounds, gradually increasing my vocabulary. It was hit and miss from one visit to the next.

One day, we drove ten miles to the nearest town. It was time to enroll for the next school year. This Oklahoma town was filled with lifted trucks. They used words like y'all, over yonder, howdy, and billfold. There was only one stoplight, which paints a picture of the population density. It was a five-minute drive from one side to the other on a green light or ten minutes on a red. The Sonic Drive-In was about as fancy as they got. If a truck was under five years old, those people were rich! They probably lived on the outskirts of town where the nice houses were. Either that or they owned a ranch. Football was practically a second religion. It wasn't uncommon to see Texas Longhorn stickers turned upside down.

I hated going there for school, but not for the reasons people thought. The sounds of shoes squeaking against the floor, lockers slamming shut, and hundreds of voices in the hall were overwhelming. Even someone walking fifty feet away was enough to get my attention. If someone dropped a book on the floor, I would react as if ET had landed. If people sang along to a high-pitched song in the car, I couldn't stand it. The vibration noise of the clippers at the barbershop drove me nuts too. I kicked and screamed my way out of there. Don't even get me started on fireworks and thunder. Loud noises were not just uncomfortable; they were physically painful. It felt like my ear canals were being stabbed again and again. I couldn't hear myself think; all I wanted to do, was make it stop. Everything was so much louder to autistic ears.

Raising a special-needs child was not for the faint of heart. It was a heavy load on my grandparents. Grandpa was on the road most of the time to make ends meet. He was home on Thursday night on the rare occasion that traffic was good. Sometimes the Hobby Lobby dispatcher was generous like that. Most weeks, he got home on Friday and left on Sunday. Grandma told me not to pig out at Sunday dinner because he had to take the leftovers to the truck. During the week, Grandma juggled her full-time teaching gig, finishing her second master's degree, and me. It was one deadline after another. She stayed up late because that was when she could do housework. She typed papers in the mornings while I got ready for school. She was constantly on the speaker phone while she was driving. She lived on Pepsi for a good reason. Luckily, she had a massive family to help her pull it off. Imagine the Reagan family on *Blue Bloods*. The only difference was that her family worked in the oilfield instead of law enforcement. She was one of eighteen kids. When she married Grandpa, he joined her family more than the other way around. He was drafted and served as an aircraft mechanic during the late Vietnam era. He was an Army drill sergeant after he left the Air Force. He never forgot how to talk like one. He got his bachelor's in psychology from OU and wanted to go further, but life got in the way. Grandpa has been many things, but he stuck with truck driving to pay the bills. His million-mile driver jacket with coffee stains said it all.

When it was just me and Grandma, I was a handful. Going out was not a simple undertaking with me in the car. I was a loaded cannon. If I made up my mind that I wanted to go somewhere, I was relentless. Going to the grocery store with Grandma was a torture treatment for her. It was difficult for me to stay still; my brain was always buzzing. Tantrums and meltdowns were a major problem. My second diagnosis was attention deficit hyperactivity disorder. ADHD was like consuming caffeine for the first time. I had an endless supply of energy. I could have run a marathon. It was hard to concentrate on anything. I felt like this all the time. I had a hard time getting to sleep and staying there. My complaint was, "I just can't turn my brain off! It's running a hundred miles an hour; I can't sleep like this!" Eventually, we ended up treating it with medication. I was prescribed several different things through the years. Some of them worked and then tapered off, some didn't do anything, and some just made the behavior worse.

If I flew too far off the handle, Grandma knew what to do. She would say, "Don't make me tell Grandpa! You know that tomorrow is Friday." My eyes got as wide as the sky. "I'm sorry, so sorry! Yes, ma'am, I'll clean my room. Please don't tell him anything!"

Grandma was willing to debate with me for a little while, but I knew the limits. If I got too much attitude, she would not hesitate to pick up that phone. Sometimes I won arguments with her, sometimes I didn't. I had to pick which battles were worth the risk.

I never tried any of that monkey business on Grandpa. With him, the first answer was the final answer. When he got angry, his old drill sergeant voice came back. That side of him was not a pretty sight. He had to be that way for most of his life. He came from a very rough place, where he had to grow up quick to defend his loved ones. His early life loosely resembled the song "A Boy Named Sue" by Johnny Cash. He knew every cop and sheriff by name before he was a teenager. He decided that the generational curse would stop with him. I am glad that he was a hard-ass. I knew how to treat people with manners and respect, thanks to Grandma and him. Grandpa played hardball when it was needed, but don't get the wrong idea about him. He knew how to be kind and gentle when the time was right.

Once a week, Grandma called one of her sisters to babysit while they went to the movies. It wasn't a matter of whether we could afford to. We couldn't afford *not* to. She and Grandpa needed that weekly break from the madness. This was one of the coping methods they used to raise a special-needs kid; movie night helped them avoid burnout. It was just as important for my well-being as it was for theirs. They made it a priority. Grandma rarely paid for movie tickets because she won them on the radio. She even won a brand-new Mustang GT with one raffle ticket! That beautiful car stayed with us a month or two before she sold it to pay off some bills. I wasn't too happy about this, but I bet Dave Ramsey would be. If something couldn't be fixed with duct tape or WD-40, it was unfixable. We weren't rich, but we weren't poor either, thanks to Grandma's savvy.

My grandparents were not alone; diagnoses like mine had become surprisingly common. When my speech therapist started out, they were taught that autism was present in one out of 12,500 kids. She saw that number change drastically. It increased to one out of every forty-five. Autism was not going anywhere anytime soon. Believe it or not, my condition wasn't entirely negative. There were some positive traits associated with it. Some sources suggested that autistic minds were physically shaped differently than the norm. For example, the hippocampus of autistic people has been reported to be enlarged in some cases. In simple terms, this was where memories were stored. I don't have a hard time believing this is plausible.

The first thing my relatives always said about my childhood is that I had an eidetic memory. They typically start with the boat commercial story. It goes like this: when the shift from standard to high-definition television was happening, there was a presentation during commercial breaks. It encouraged antenna users to buy the all-new HD television box that they were offering. It was a constantly played commercial with a lot of information. Somehow the topic came up while we were on Grandpa's Skeeter boat. We were fishing on Lake Thunderbird. The legend goes that I recited the entire presentation, including the voice tones, perfectly. My family gets a huge kick out of that one. Uncle David, or "Dave-on," as he got called until I took speech therapy, didn't like it when I started parroting him. He often said things that he didn't want to have repeated. If he was brave enough to utter his controversial opinions around me, they would eventually get broadcast in one way or another.

David had a catchphrase. His go-to response to something he disagreed with was, "That's crazy talk." I think he learned to say this because he knew that Grandma would get madder than a wet hen if he let out a curse word and got me repeating it. David's efforts were moot when I adopted his catchphrase as my own around teachers. Both of my grandparents were tied up one day, so they called Uncle David to pick me up. Shortly after, a white Toyota pickup pulled up to Krouch Early Childhood Center. Uncle David waltzed in and began filling out some paperwork. I could hear his voice a hundred miles away, so I dropped everything I was doing in a jiffy. "Dave-on!" I yelled, running down the hallway. The teacher knew the drill at this point, so she didn't even try to keep up with me. She casually strolled out of the classroom, expecting me to already be in the principal's office. Sure enough, I was, but not for the reason she thought. I could hear her heels clicking against the floor as she stormed our way. Her jaw practically dropped to the floor when she saw how I was acting around David. I was sitting still and doing everything that he told me, just like I should. Her facial expression said a thousand words. "How is he doing that," she must have thought. She and David introduced themselves. She saw the pieces coming together. "You're the 'Uncle Dave-on' guy?" Those two went on to have a lengthy discussion about my ways. It was pretty one-sided. David definitely didn't sign up for a scolding that day, but he got it, nonetheless. "I told you not to repeat everything I say!"

Autism did not come with a road map or an expiration date. We had no way of knowing when or if I was going to develop. It could have been a temporary speed bump or a lifelong struggle. Blending in and functioning in society wasn't a guarantee. There was a slim chance that my grandparents would have to be my long-term caretakers well into adulthood. Learning how to live in a society of neurotypicals would be a lifelong process. Something I admire them for is that they never gave up on me. No matter how difficult it got, that wasn't an option for them.

CHAPTER TWO — **Train of Thought**

I loved December for several reasons. I didn't need to check for sweaty armpits as soon as I walked out the door. That alone made it a wonderful time of the year. Oh yeah, that big holiday themed around gifts and candy was nice too. The last day of school before break was reserved for the big party. Everyone was told to wear pajamas and bring a blanket to sit on. Our backpacks were stuffed to the brims with snacks and candy. The whole class split into two rooms. I raced inside and saw that the chairs and desks were gone. The teachers had stayed late the night before, decorating the room. Everyone's homemade Christmas ornaments were hanging from the ceiling. A squeaking noise rolled in from the hallway. We laid out our blankets as the principal plugged in the TV. It was bungeed to a rolling cart. She got out a blue and yellow DVD. I knew what we were watching. Someone hit the lights and closed the blinds.

The Polar Express will always be my favorite Christmas film. The deep roar as the train pulls up gave me goosebumps. This movie may not have been the latest and greatest in animation, but the soundtrack was pure gold. When I watched *The Polar Express*, I stuck around until the final credits were over. I might have been nerdy for doing this, but I didn't care. The music during the credits was the best part for me. I didn't need the visuals to tell what part of the movie was being played. I remembered the entire soundtrack. Autistic boys liking trains is a cliché; it is almost expected. This is one of the few stereotypes that I affirmed in my life.

Sound was much more than just some air molecules vibrating. Audio was an entire experience for an autistic person. The deep rumble of those train pistons and railroad tracks was something I could feel. Audio was euphoric. Certain music brought back every detail of an experience. Many of my obsessions began because of some sort of audio experience.

Grandpa shut off the semi-truck that Friday and came home with a big box on his shoulder. It was a train set. He and Grandma wanted to get me interested in something besides television. That mission was accomplished; I became a train fanatic. The cars were hand-painted. The engine had many intricate parts and made smoke as it rolled around the track. He eventually bought a plywood table to place my train set on. My bedroom had wood paneling that gave it a rustic, vintage look. I had a captain's bed with storage underneath. It looked like a bunk bed that had been repurposed. I had to jump or climb up onto the mattress. There were several rows of drawers, with one big cabinet door in the middle. I could fit into the door, which led to an enclosed space under the bed. When my siblings visited, my oldest sister and I had a secret club under my bed that we entered through the cabinet door. It was honestly just an opportunity to trash talk our younger sister and color with crayons on the wall. We masterminded scavenger hunts to keep ourselves occupied. My siblings came to visit several times per year but, most of the time, I lived in my own bubble. I was responsible for entertaining myself. I think this is part of where my creative imagination came from. I created a miniature world in my head.

On Saturday, Grandpa and I went to Shawnee. Going to town for anything but school, work, or church was rare. I tagged along just to get off of our property for a few hours. I kicked the Pepsi cans and donut wrappers out of the way and climbed into the Blazer. Grandma made us drive with the windows down because of the cigarette smell. Johnny Cash was blasting over the radio as always. We came around a bend, and the Blazer shuttered. It began as a subtle shake and began vibrating powerfully as we approached a bridge. If I didn't know better, I would have thought it was an earthquake. Leaves paraded off the bridge like a tidal wave. A powerful roar rattled the windshield. Bright lights were glistening off the tree line. Grandpa's coffee nearly slopped out of his cup. Just then, a freight train thundered over the bridge. It was going way too fast for us to hear the clicking. We only heard a deep roar. He slowed down for a second look after we cleared the bridge. When the train was gone, he put the Blazer in gear and proceeded to town. I yanked my seat belt off and laid the seat down so I could turn around. "But Grandpa, wait! Train!" I pointed at the bridge. Most of the time, he would have kept going, business as usual. On this particular day, though, he looked at his watch and shrugged. We pulled into a driveway and parked. "What are we doing here?" He turned the radio off and crunched his cigarette butt into the ground. He cleared his throat and shifted into reverse. "You wanted to see a train, didn't you?" I didn't know what he meant by that, so I stayed quiet. I did not want to look a gift horse in the mouth. We drove down a bumpy road that led to a trailer park. I had no clue where we were. We passed the trailers and drove into an industrial area with graffiti on the walls. He appeared to be looking for something as we cruised around the lot. Oil tanks and storage pallets towered over us. He made a left and drove all the way down to the railroad tracks at the back of the lot. A freight train was stopped, still hissing from the heat.

Two men emerged from it and appeared to be closing shop for the day. Grandpa walked up to them and asked if we could take a closer look. The operators smirked and shrugged their shoulders, saying, "Well, we're leaving, but she's all yours." I ran up the steps like a spider monkey. The whistle didn't work but at least I can say that I pulled the string. I will never forget the excitement of seeing the real deal. It was forever etched on my brain. I remembered it and drew it multiple times.

Many outsiders wondered why I was wired to be so obsessive. I was asked countless times, "How can you focus on one subject for years at a time? Do you not go mad?" The best way I could describe it was by comparing it to falling in love. It was much like a first crush and all of the emotions that come with it. A river bubbled through my veins. My pupils dilated like a camera lens. It was the first thing I thought about in the morning. Seeing it was enough to make a bad day good. My friends were going to learn the juicy details whether they wanted to know them or not. Nobody could get me to shut up about it. My entire world was incredible. That emotional high people got when they heard their crush's name is how I felt about trains. That feeling of infatuation really did last months and years at a time. When I got interested in something, I became a fanatic about it. Every day, there was something new to learn about trains. That dopamine rush of excitement got renewed on a regular basis. It was like I was watching *The Polar Express* for the first time, all over again. I was very focused and directed in my interests. I might've changed my mind, but I wouldn't change it from one day to the next. I would think it out; I worked my way gradually down the path of change.

I was assigned a full-time aide at school. First grade was a hard time academically. My aide was familiar with the difficulties because her grandson was also autistic. She had read some books about the subject and learned how to use an autistic person's quirks to help them get ahead. She did this with me. I sketched several different types of trains for her. I explained what type of train each one was and how it worked. I drew a diagram of a steam locomotive and lectured for hours about how a steam engine works. Some people at the school were concerned about my intellectual ability because I was falling behind in reading and writing. She saw something that the other teachers didn't. She bought toy trains and brought them to school. When she handed them to me, I got very excited and gladly talked to her. She saw that I had the ability to succeed academically, but I was just smart about different things than most people. She knew I had what it took to learn how to read and write. She just needed to get my brain to remember words the way I remembered trains.

She made lesson plans that worked well with my autistic abilities. She made me part of the learning process; I was allowed to have input. She wrote her name on the assignment papers, along with mine. She used a different language to teach me than she did with the rest of the class. She started with train-related sentences and gradually increased their difficulty. She made it a competition. It was a badge of honor for me to finish my portion of the worksheet before she finished hers. She used flash cards taped to poster boards and other visual methods to get me to learn. When I took my spelling tests, I remembered the cards more than the actual words themselves. This method did, in fact, work. With enough repetition, the dots started connecting in my mind. She made a copy of the flashcards and sent them to Grandma. By working together, they taught me to read and write. Over time, I actually started progressing ahead of the other students.

Teaching an autistic person was difficult. I didn't always behave well, nor did I always want to do the work. The personal attention I received made me flourish. She saw so many autistic kids who could have flourished like I did but, unfortunately, they didn't. Sadly, knowing that their children were autistic, many parents didn't give the personal attention and support needed for success. The parents thought it was hopeless. Because I got all that attention from Grandma, I was able to live up to my fullest potential. So many teachers and adults were not willing to warm up to kids with autism or any other kinds of problems. They were often afraid that they were incapable of helping because those children were different and presented unique challenges. It angered people like my aide because she knew that they were capable and valuable. I wholeheartedly believe that I met and even exceeded the bar that she set for me. Others were unsure of where the bar should be set. She, on the other hand, set it high to make sure I excelled. I started believing that I had what it took to make it in school. It was easy because she and Grandma believed in me first.

CHAPTER THREE — Liberty to Draw

N o one saw things quite as I did. It was frustrating. I did not fully understand autism yet, but I could feel a divide. I knew that my thought patterns were significantly different from those of everyone around me. I couldn't articulate my thoughts and feelings very well. Dialogue was challenging because my autistic mind wasn't wired that way. When I spoke, I was often misinterpreted.

I was a visual person; it was the deepest essence of who I was. I thought and processed things visually. My memory worked like a visual Rolodex. It started with the earliest thing I could remember. It went on for infinity and ended at the current date. I could reel this imaginary Rolodex back anytime I wanted. Each card played a highlight reel when my mind scrolled to it. It looked like a slideshow or instant replay on a sports telecast. Every single card on the Rolodex was unique. They had tabs to categorize them into major life events. I had categories for trains, family, music, and many other things. The way my brain worked had an official term. Many people referred to it as an "eidetic memory." When I saw something or took in information, my brain took snapshots for the Rolodex.

My memory could be the greatest thing ever or the worst. I remembered what clothes people wore, what cars they drove, what they said, and much more. These were not things I intentionally thought about, but nonetheless, I did remember them. I was proud of this skill. I didn't get to show it off often because it made people very uncomfortable. I had to pretend that I didn't remember things to avoid freaking them out. I can't count the times I did this to keep a conversation going and avoid uncomfortable situations.

My brain didn't respond with answers; It responded with images. It had worked that way since the beginning. Since I processed things visually, it only made sense to start communicating visually as well. This is what led me to become an artist. My drawings helped bridge the gap between the outside world and me. Art began as a means to explain and validate myself. I had a knack for it from an early age. It was like breathing. I spent a lot of time doing it. People took notice and started to understand me better. I liked the positive attention, so I started doing it more often. Drawing allowed me to freely communicate with everybody else without barriers.

On weekends, Grandpa pulled all the cars out of the garage. He cleaned them up and then took off fishing. I grabbed a giant barrel of colored chalk and got to work. My drawings were massive. They spanned from one side of the garage to the other. I didn't look around very much while I worked; I didn't have to. I got on my knees and sketched. It looked as if I was following a guide or tracing something, but I wasn't. I had the entire drawing planned in my head beforehand. I could see where the train's cowcatcher, wheels, and smokestack were supposed to be in perspective. I saw it in my head as a grid. I used cracks in the concrete and wall beams to section the room into grid squares. I moved around on the floor to the grid square that I was drawing. One square at a time, I sketched. At the end of the day, they all connected into one cohesive piece. We all stood back and gazed at the finished product. Grandpa asked me, "How did you do this when you couldn't see the whole thing at once?" I shrugged my shoulders and pointed at my forehead. I said, "I draw what I see in here! It's like a grid. Isn't that what everyone does?" He and Grandma were both shaking their heads and smiling in amusement. "No, they don't. You have a gift."

I took out a library book about the Statue of Liberty and tried to draw the statue exactly as I saw it. The first attempt was not very good. I tried again. I used my mental grid method and got the proportions right this time. It was progress, but something was still off. The picture looked too flat. I didn't want to be a cartoon-style artist. Since this skill was my bridge to the outside world, I had to excel at it. I read the book countless times and fell in love with New York. I had to know everything that there was to know about Lady Liberty. Just like that, the obsession began.

My school district had a system called "accelerated reading tests." This was their way of motivating children to read. A weekly parade through the hallways celebrated the highest performers. They also gave prizes as incentives for taking AR tests. I read every single library book about the Statue of Liberty and then some. They even had books sent to me from the higher-level schools in the district. I ordered several from the public library every time Grandma took me there. My teachers attempted to sway me toward reading other books but to no avail. I had my mind set on this subject, and there was no turning back. That was part of the obsessive behavior rooted in my autism. Forget about trains; Lady Liberty was here to stay.

In a matter of months, I could take AR tests for books that I had not even read yet. I knew every detail. One of the teachers asked me about it, and I spouted everything. I knew that she was a gift to the United States by France. The name of the artist who masterminded the project was Fredric Bartholdi. It was built in Paris and shipped in 214 crates to Bedloe's Island, where a military fort once stood. That fort is where the star-shaped pedestal came from. When I say that I did not Google search these facts, I am not kidding. I remembered these facts quite well. All I needed was a stack of paper, a cardboard box, and a tape dispenser to create a paper model. However, a replica wasn't good enough for me. I had to go to New York and draw it from life.

I rose from the sheets one day and saw my paper statue staring back at me. The smell of bacon hugged my face as I turned the corner. My folks made stern expressions at each other. They were hiding something, but I wasn't awake enough to care. Grandma shook her head and said, "I'll take care of all that later, okay?" Grandpa threw his hands up in response. "All right, well, I already told Hobby Lobby I'm using my vacation time." I grabbed a plate and retreated to the TV. Grandma was too busy to nag me to get ready. She was dragging luggage bags around.

Right after sunrise, Grandpa knocked on the screen door, pointing at his watch. Red lights were glistening off the telephone wires. I could hear the bus coming as I sprinted down to the road. By the skin of my teeth, I made it. At the end of the school day, the intercom speaker came on. "Could you send Joseph Perry to the office to check out, please?" I got in the car and saw a stack of papers crunched under Grandma's purse. They were ticket receipts. "Round trip to New York for three." Grandma told me to grab my jacket when we got home because I was going to need it.

We drove through the fog to the airport. It was pitch-black outside except for runway lights. There was a greenish-blue halo above the OKC skyline. I stopped my portable CD player to switch disks. I had had enough Credence Clearwater Revival for a while. Grandpa traded me for a black and yellow disk from the console. It was Neil Diamond. I still have a sentimental attachment to Neil's music to this day. We had an entire row of seats to ourselves on the plane. Grandpa was on the right side, while Grandma and I got the two left-side seats.

After what seemed like an eternity, the water came into view. Suburbs emerged from the fog. There was a green smudge with a yellow smudge above it, but there was no way to tell what it was. I had never seen this many people at one time. We got a taxi the old-fashioned way and headed toward the buzz of the city. We merged onto the interstate, which led uphill. We kept going up, all the way to a massive truss bridge. Red construction cranes were on our right and water on our left. We finally reached the summit of the hill. Slowly but surely, everything rose into view. The clouds opened up, letting the sunshine through. It was almost too perfect, as if a cinematic curtain had been opened. Over the trees was that iconic yellow torch flame. She looked so far away but so close at the same time. The motion blur created an optical illusion of her walking. I suppose it gets lonesome up there, so who could blame her? We stayed on the New Jersey side. The hotel room was high enough to see Ellis Island and the statue's torch on the horizon.

Our door clicked shut just before morning. Grandpa had gone downstairs. He wasn't fooling anybody; he was heading straight for the nearest coffee machine. Sure enough, I saw an orange Hobby Lobby cap walking the block with a smoke trail behind him.

I opened the curtains and grabbed a legal pad from Grandpa's laptop bag. I looked straight ahead at the statue and drew what I saw. I kept at it until Grandma got up. This sketch was the best one I had ever done up to that point.

We ended up at three or four places before we figured out public transit. On the bright side, I got a good dose of Hanna Montana advertisements. The Black-Eyed Peas were hyping up their *Energy Never Dies* album set to release that June. We boarded and set our sights on Liberty Island. I got out my sketchbook. I was ecstatic to take it to Liberty Island and see how accurately I had sketched it.

I kept stopping throughout the tour. "Wait, I have to draw that!" I sketched the outlines of every exhibit. We walked by a glass porthole that allowed us to see the statue's framework above. The tour guide passed over it and led the group outside. "But wait, you forgot something," I said, pointing upward. Grandma buried her face in embarrassment while Grandpa buckled up for the lecture. "Doesn't the structural design remind you of the Eiffel Tower? There is a reason for that," I asserted. Gustave Eiffel designed the statue's framework. He engineered it, so the copper sheets were independently attached to the framework. This allows parts of the statue to flex under high winds instead of breaking apart under the stress. The torch can sway five inches or more. Everyone held awkward eye contact with me, including the tour guide. I didn't know what a know-it-all I was at that age. "This kid knows more about this thing than I do. Is he trying to take my job or something?" Despite resistance from my grandparents, we went to Liberty Island three times that week.

I filled the legal pad with drawings and was then content to go home. I hung onto that pad for years. I spent a lot of time teaching myself to draw better and more accurately. I re-drew the statue I don't know how many times. I lost count, but it must have been in the thousands. I challenged myself to draw each fold of the robe and the proportions exactly like the real thing.

I was not content with my drawings until I got them accurate to life. I was very secretive with my artwork until I got it to a place of utmost perfection. When a drawing was done, I walked to the kitchen to ask Grandma what her first impression was. Before ever showing it to her, I had already decided that the drawing was good. I didn't do this for validation or praise. I mostly did it to double-check and vet my drawings. I only wanted to show my polished work to the outside world. If my grandparents liked a drawing, that meant I was ready to start showing it to people. I brought the pad to school, church, and just about everywhere else. I used it as a conversation starter. It deeply irritated me when people saw unfinished drawings. I spoke up and grabbed the pad. "Wait, wait, don't look at that one! That's not done yet. This next one is done, but not that one."

The better I became at drawing the statue, the more confident I became in my art skillset. I stretched my talent even further by copying family portraits. I was given a set of small canvases from a garage sale. I cleaned them up and got out my pastels. I created a series of about ten pieces based on my legal pad sketches from New York. I spent an entire day or more on each one. I got them all done and put them in the family yard sale. Two were bought by family members and one by my third-grade teacher. These were the first three art pieces I ever sold. Technically, I had just become a professional artist.

CHAPTER FOUR — Friendship Forecast

I spent most of my childhood around adults. I liked having adult-like conversations because I was familiar with the process. I mostly parroted what my grandparents said. I got into a spirited debate with a relative about politics once. She asked me, "Do you have any idea what we're talking about here?" I shrugged my shoulders and said, "Not really. I just heard that guy in the brown suit talking about it while I was waiting for church to start. What are we talking about?" I guess I earned that eye roll she gave me shortly afterward. I was frustrated with a teacher on one occasion when I said, "I don't perform well for those who give me grief." Since I dressed like a nerd, I reckon I had to act the part too. I had become so comfortable around adults and their conversations that I fell out of touch with kids my own age. Quite honestly, interacting with my peers seemed a little scary.

Adults were simple and to the point; my peers, not so much. It was a guessing game figuring out what would set them off. Often, socializing with other kids was just too much. When the school day was done, I had a sense of relief. I didn't have to wear a mask anymore. I could be a true introvert like I was born to be. It's not that I didn't like people but socializing was a lot of work for me. My ability to socialize worked like a battery. On a full charge, I felt great and chatty. I didn't mind putting in the work during this phase. Some people drained the battery quicker than others. It was nothing personal, but certain people were more challenging to engage with than others. Once the battery got depleted, I just couldn't do it anymore. The battery needed to be recharged before it could work at its fullest potential again. This happened when my brain was at rest.

My peers and I had nothing in common. My attitude was, "If I don't want or need anything, why should I talk to these people?" Holding friendships seemed like it would be too much work. I didn't understand the concept of small talk. I was willing to talk about the Statue of Liberty or my drawings, but there wasn't much else on the menu. The other kids had little to say to me, and I had little to say to them. There was an exception to that rule. One kid in my school was tolerable.

He was sitting in the corner of the auditorium one day. I walked over and asked how his place fared during the recent storm. "Good. You know, I'm pretty sure I've seen one. A...a tornado. I think I saw one. I saw something. You know, they said on the news that it had winds over a hundred miles an hour. The one I saw anyway. What's your name?"

"Joey, you?"

"Uh, Andrew."

He asked, "Do you know exactly how a tornado works, huh, Joey?" I shook my head. When he started thinking really hard, he tilted his head slightly and put his hands together. He talked in a flat, toneless voice like I did. He said, "Well, exactly, it happens because of air colliding. Warm air from the Gulf of Mexico collides with cold air from the Rocky Mountains. That's why we're in 'tornado alley.' All of that creates a spin. See, like this." He reached into his backpack and got out a clear plastic tube. It contained soapy water with a picture of the Oklahoma plains inside. "This is my tornado bottle." He spun it and set it on the ground. Sure enough, there was a small "tornado" inside. He handed it to me. I tried spinning it, but it just sloshed around. He said, "Exactly, you have to do it fast, like really fast." Andrew was the school-wide weatherman. Teachers asked him what the forecast was. He could recite the weatherman on TV verbatim. If they said it was going to be a high of 75 degrees with a ten-mile-per-hour wind, that is exactly what he repeated. The teachers were quite amused.

Andrew was the first non-adult I could relate to. I could tell he was different from most of my peers. We gradually started hanging out more often with time. "You know, my Grandma usually takes me to McDonald's before church on Wednesday. You should meet us there."

"Yeah, I'll talk to my mom." As we walked in, he raced to the door to hold it open. "I got here first!" In his eyes, everything was a sport. He invented competitions in everyday life. Who would get on the bus first? Who would get packed up first? When he lost a round of bowling, he acted like the world was coming to an end! He jumped up and down and made funny faces to mess everyone else up. When it was his turn to bowl, he smirked and yelled out, "Oh, watch...THIS! Buddy ole pal!" He had a unique vocabulary, that's for sure. Few people in the entire world made me laugh like Andy could.

His stories were different from most other people's stories. His facial expressions and overall demeanor got involved when he told a story. The only word I can think of is animated. Everything he said and did, he did with extreme intensity. I related to that. None of my other peers seemed to think this way.

While we ran around the playground tunnels in McDonald's, our parents compared notes. They encouraged each other through hard times and learned a lot. One year after the next, they started treating me like a member of the family. That's just who they were. They have always been there to help my grandparents and me through whatever life has thrown at us.

I hitched a ride with Andrew's folks to an arcade one day. We stopped by his mother's office. All eyes were planted on the TV. It could have been game day or just a weather thing. It was hard to tell. The TV beeped three times and played dramatic music. "This is a News 9 weather update!" The room got quiet. A gruff voice came from the hall as muddy boots clinked on the floor. "Well, do we need our lawn chairs today or what?" The room got a good chuckle out of that. Everyone knew what he meant. The broadcast showed radar readings. Green areas were okay, but red was not a great thing. Magenta was the worst of all. There were magenta dots all over the map. "We are looking at a very powerful supercell here, folks!" Someone yelled, "Ah, it's going northeast like it always does! We're good!" Everyone went about their day as usual.

Andy wasn't buying it. He kept trying to get his mom's attention, but they were all distracted in the breakroom. We both saw what appeared to be a big mountain outside. Actually, it was a series of mountains. Lightning bolts wrapped around them like shoelaces. Those were no mountains; they were thunderheads. They looked so fluffy and innocent at first. The sun faded, and the sky turned a dark blue-gray. The clouds had some colors that I had never seen before. There were some greens and even some deep violets. It looked like huge marshmallows were swirling in a pot of water. The sky was angrier than a mule chewing on bumblebees. I could see trees swaying on the horizon, but it was still calm at the office.

His mom came back to the lobby and said, "What is so important?" The wind hit the building like a slap in the face. The lobby door exploded open. "See, I told you to watch the weather!" We all scrambled out and headed to one of their friends' houses. They had an underground storm cellar in their garage. We didn't have much time. I could barely hear the weatherman yelling on the radio. The static got so loud that we couldn't hear him anymore. Lightning must have hit a transformer because a bunch of lights went out. We raced up a hill and into the garage.

We couldn't see the whole thing because of the trees, but we saw something dark pointed downward. It was so far away, though, that I didn't understand Andy's panic. "It looks like it's miles away from here. It isn't even moving," I said. We went down into the cellar. One of the ladies swilled her tea and said, "If it looks like it's standing still, it's probably coming toward you. You just don't know it yet." I heard a roar coming. It sounded like the blowers at a car wash or a freight train passing. Hail pounded the roof. We had to stay down there for quite a while. This was the start of a lifelong friendship.

We did everything together after second grade. Andrew would always be my best friend. I had the same group of friends for most of my life. Trust was a big deal for me. I knew that Andy wouldn't put me down for being different than the other kids. I never had to worry about that with him.

My friendship with Andrew opened my eyes. I started to get a sense of how wide the autism spectrum truly is. I had a lot of things in common with Andy, but there were some distinct differences too. He was raised with a sibling, which was an environment in polar opposition to mine. He was accustomed to playing with others. He was always around people, while I wasn't. He wasn't on the exact same spot on the autism spectrum that I was. He had some differences that I didn't fully understand. He started talking faster and louder when he was excited about something. He also had some repetitive tendencies. For instance, he tended to start his sentences with the word "exactly." My initial reaction to these was common. I got frustrated and a little annoyed. Over time, I had to learn how to turn my frustration into understanding. I was forced to get out of my shell and change to maintain this friendship. I haven't always been the greatest friend I could be. You will learn about that in a few chapters. However, I have probably grown more through my friendship with him than in any other way.

I looked at Andy in the beginning much like others looked at me. People tend to be annoyed by behaviors they are unfamiliar with. We fear the unknown. This is not exclusive to autism at all; it is actually engrained in our human nature. Knowledge gives us comfort. We want to know what to expect. Going into a situation blind is very uncomfortable. The more I understood Andy, the more I started to understand myself.

Chapter Five — Geek Reflex

I needed a new obsession to entertain myself. I stayed with the Statue of Liberty for a few years, but it was becoming a little dull. I had hit a dead end. My obsessions started coming and going in waves. I would be crazy about something for a month and then taper off. Sometimes an obsession lasted for a year, sometimes for several years. At some point, I always ran into the same problem. I kept hitting dead ends. I collected everything imaginable and went down every rabbit hole. I was running out of facts to learn and things to do. When I had nothing left to learn about the subject, I started losing interest in it. This was a problem because I didn't know what else to do with my life. I needed a long-term interest.

I saw the Pixar movie *Cars* at the theater one Friday. I had never seen anything so wild, chaotic, and mesmerizing at the same time. The noise of a racecar engine had authority to it, like a beast attacking its prey. The cars were a blur. They demanded my shock, awe, and respect. What drew me in most of all was the constant state of curiosity. I could never know everything about car racing. This distinguished racing from all of my other obsessions.

One Saturday, we drove a couple of towns over like always. It was the day that Grandma spent with her mother. Everyone and their dog came to that house on Sundays, no matter what. Saturdays on the other hand, were much quieter. Most of my great aunts stayed busy at garage sales. First thing in the morning, we took Great Grandma to the beauty shop. While she was getting her hair done, we went to Walmart for groceries. This was my opportunity to get a Hot Wheels car. They were inexpensive, so I usually got one every week. Before long, one car per week was not cutting it. I started vacuuming Great-Grandma's house every week to earn spending money. The collection grew faster. In the blink of an eye, I filled a 100-car collector's case. I laid eyes on a Hot Wheels racetrack set and had to have it. One after another, my collection started adding up.

I ended up with hundreds of orange track pieces and nearly a thousand cars. I started toting them with me in a tub every weekend. I stacked books, boxes, pillows, furniture, and whatever else I could find to build my tracks. I got a camcorder to start documenting them. I liked to give the viewers a nerd lesson about the architectural design before racing the car. Often, the track wasn't stable enough with pillows alone, so I used wooden boards and balanced weight on each side to keep it from flexing. When the car jumped too high and flipped over, I raised the ramp to slow the car down. I loved challenging myself to solve these brainteasers. My track layouts had humble beginnings, but ended up being 100+ feet long. I downloaded Windows Movie Maker and edited my videos. That was when my first YouTube channel was born.

My uncle Kurt took me to a live car race near Tulsa. The noise was overwhelming, and we left early that day. The next time, I could tolerate the noise slightly better with headphones. I started going with him to local dirt tracks to shoot vlogs. He had been a crew member on a dirt-modified racing team for a few seasons. As I got older, the noise bothered me less. With time, I was able to stay in the grandstands with him for the entire event. He was very gracious in dealing with my autistic sound sensitivity.

He also took me to my first NASCAR race. We went to the Samsung Mobile 500 at Texas Motor Speedway. I saw corporate ads, TV graphics, merchandise, and signage surrounding the stadium. There were thousands of people camping and tailgating. The air smelled like tire rubber and barbecue sauce. Most people's breaths smelled like beer. The teams took the tarps off the cars and let them shine in the Texas sun. Forty-three fire-breathing monsters fired up. The next three hours were absolutely incredible. NASCAR was everything I dreamed it would be. I fell in love with that atmosphere. My longest-lasting obsession had begun.

Uncle Kurt got me an electric slot car set for Christmas. The cars had guide pins that fit into grooves in the track. Two metal strips conducted power to the cars. The speed controllers looked like pistols. I had to slow down for corners, or I wrecked out of the track. I took the set home and kept it upstairs. A while later, I upgraded to digital slot cars. This allowed me to run multiple cars and switch lanes.

Grandma gave me free rein over the upstairs room to build my geeky masterpiece. I created a Grand-Prix-style track layout up there. I printed a bunch of logos, taped them to cardboard, and placed them around the track to convince YouTube viewers that I had sponsors. I taped posters, magazines, and other racing imagery to the walls surrounding the track. I got out my old Lego set to create grandstands, garages, pit boxes, and more. What most people did not understand about my slot car track was that it was more than a toy racetrack. It was a miniature world that my mind could get lost in. My imagination made short movie clips out of what it saw. I imagined what the intro music for the broadcast would sound like, what the opening scene would be, and what camera angles I would use. I could see the pistons moving and the air particles flowing over the cars. I could imagine the wall and catch-fences rumbling. I could sense the suspension compressing as the cars charged into the corners. My mind saw everything. My creation was an attempt at making that vision become reality. It never quite measured up to how I imagined it, but I did the best I could.

Once I finished the track, I was ready to host competitions. I invited friends and family to come upstairs and race. I came up with catchy names for these events. I created brochures and PowerPoint presentations in anticipation. The first big race happened when people came to my birthday party. I had it all planned out. I printed out spreadsheets to determine who would face off against whom. I gave out brochures and told people that they could win a prize. Planning this slot car competition was the most exciting thing in the world. My only anxiety about it was losing. I didn't want to give up the prize, namely, my Sonic gift card.

When the big day came, I shined up the slot cars and made sure the track was ready. I pulled up my PowerPoint presentation on my grandparent's computer and waited. Six or ten kids showed up. I got down to business. Rule number one was that if someone crashed out, they would say, "Caution." This meant that everyone had to stop and allow them to put their car back on track. Rule number two prohibited people from obstructing the camera. My biggest pet peeve was having the footage partially cut off. This meant that, if cars were moving, people were not. Last but not least, there was a ten-strike policy. If someone crashed ten times, they were disqualified for "impeding the racing."

Everybody sat on the couches and grabbed their controllers. I lined up the cars, hit record, and started counting down. One of them took off early as a joke. I did not take it that way. I paused everything and exclaimed, "Stop, you're going to chip the paint! These slot cars are rare. It took me three weeks to save up and another three to find them in mint condition." There was an awkward pause. I deleted that recording and started over. Some of the bystanders shook their heads. I didn't understand why; it all made perfect sense to me.

The race finally started. I sat in the stairwell and kept a tally of the laps on my clipboard. I enforced the rules with an iron fist. It just ground my gears if there wasn't a procedure. Driving slot cars around the track aimlessly made no sense to me. There had to be order. Halfway through the first heat race, someone wiped out. All of the cars stopped except one. I put my hand onto the track as a barrier. I was dead serious when I said, "You...are required to stop!" Some of my friends thought it was a bit ridiculous to take a miniature car race so seriously. I saw it as a legitimate championship. Some rolled their eyes when I called it that.

One guy mumbled, "Well, at least the food is good here." The guy next to him whispered, "Yeah, it's all right. Joey is so bossy during his races! Jeez!" I didn't know how to respond, so I pretended that I didn't hear them. We kept going in a tournament-style elimination system until we got down to two cars. I was excited. "All right, it all comes down to this! This is the final race!" By now, most people had gone downstairs or left. I introduced the two finalists to the camera. "Fifty laps! Winner takes all!" I got out my wallet and set my Sonic gift card in the middle of the track. I also added a $10 bill to sweeten the deal. Everybody looked at each other and started giggling. One of the racers said, "really? All of this just for that? It's all yours, Andrew. I'm going downstairs for cake." He patted Andy's shoulder and walked out of the frame.

A few seconds later, Grandma yelled, "Joey, come down here! We're ready to do the candles and cut the cake." I exclaimed, "But why? The race isn't over yet!" The other racer threw his hands up and hysterically said, "Yes, it is!" The other kids started laughing. Grandma chuckled a little bit herself. She motioned for me to hurry up. I mumbled under my breath, "Great, since there's no winner, I can't use this footage for my YouTube channel!" I stopped the recording and slouched down the stairs.

I went to school and talked about my slot car track with anyone who would listen. I sketched technical diagrams in my school binder to explain visually. My poor special education teacher heard all about it. I drew a racetrack on the whiteboard and held up two erasers to demonstrate the cars. She tried to act interested to be nice, but that confused me. I couldn't figure out why she was asking questions and engaging, then ending the conversation thirty seconds later. I couldn't decipher the other body language signs like slouching in the chair, looking around, and glancing at the door. It never dawned on me that people said certain things while thinking another. Life was so sudden and unpredictable.

Since my classmates were sick of hearing about it, I planned to start an online community. I was geeky enough to find a corner of the internet called "Google Sites." It was a service that allowed nerds like me to create websites for free. This was back in the era of dial-up internet. Grandma had to tell me to log off when she wanted to use the telephone. My first website was called "Joe's Slots." The logo looked like a kid had finger-painted it because that's exactly what I did. I boldly claimed that this site was a place where "we bring you the thrills and chills of slot car racing." I posted a schedule and had a page dedicated to rules and regulations. I had big plans to start an interactive blog section with profiles for each racer. I started the race broadcasts from that day forward by yelling, "We're live here at the Joe's Slots Speedway!"

I thought I had launched the next iCarly. I expected it to be a big hit. The first problem was that I did not know a thing about web design. All text was the same size but in several typefaces. Don't even get me started on the animations. It seemed like I had a love affair with the caps lock button.

I logged in one day to check the Joe's Slots message board. I was notified that there were new comments. I was stoked to see what they were. I went to the site editor and scrolled to the bottom. Somebody from school had found the website. Comments started buzzing wildly both on my site and on my YouTube channel. They were all posted by anonymous accounts. Very few of them were positive.

I didn't understand why my peers were becoming annoyed with me. I was bossy during the races to give everybody a fair chance of winning. I hoped to put on a good, competitive race for the YouTube audience. The other kids did not see it that way. I started to get the sense that I was no longer the normal one. Maybe they were the normal ones the whole time, and I needed to change. Perhaps I needed to be more accommodating to the differences between them and me to make it easier for them to deal with. My time of ignorant bliss was slowly running out. My hobbies and interests would have to take a back seat for a little while. I had bigger problems to worry about. This was just a minor setback, or so I thought.

CHAPTER SIX — Liturgy of the Disconnect

G randma was very involved in our church, especially when Grandpa was on the road. This meant I had to go with her. Growing up this way meant a few things. A juicy steak always smelled the best on days it was forbidden. Sunday was a day of rest, but homework was an exception. I wasn't a pastor's kid, but I might as well have been. I was as close to it as I could get.

The church I grew up in had arched windows. They towered over the crowd. The ceilings were crazy high. They had elegant chandeliers and big speakers hanging. Little bits of incense smoke shimmered in the light rays. Everything echoed inside. The pews were made of stained wood. The church services were always a huge event, and hundreds of people attended. Everything about this place was a big deal.

When the church service was halfway over, Grandpa ran to the restroom. Grandma got up to carry some baskets to the front of the church. While they were gone, the pastor raised both arms into the air. He said, "Let us offer each other the sign of peace." After this, I was expected to shake hands and make conversation with people I didn't know. I looked around and tried to copy everyone else. A middle-aged couple stood behind me in nice clothes. I turned around and went through the motions. The man snapped his fingers. He cleaned his glasses as he crouched down to my eye level. "Hey, kid! You know you're supposed to look people in the eye when you shake their hands. It's disrespectful not to!" I nodded along and did as I was told. The next week, he chuckled and said, "Gee, kid! Do you ever blink? You're going to freak people out staring at them like that!" I saw the eye rolls and snarky laughter. "Sir, didn't you tell me to hold eye contact because it's a respect thing? I'm confused. What you're saying now is highly hypocritical based on what you said last week." His wife rolled her eyes and said, "Are you seriously talking back to him? Who do you think you are? Where's your Grandma?" They waved her over and said, "Deal with your disrespectful kid here!" The only words I could get out were, "She is a liar!"

Grandma smiled and walked me out to the car. I slapped the empty car seat and yelled, "Why didn't you do anything? Do you seriously believe her over me?" Grandma started the car and replied, "I will talk to them another time! I can't make a scene during church. Speaking of which, you better cool your jets when your grandfather gets out here. You know he doesn't tolerate arguing. He's in a crabby mood today, so we'll have to talk about this later." She locked the car doors and waited for Grandpa. After church ended, we circled through the main parking lot. The couple was walking toward my window. My chest tightened with angst as my heart raced a hundred miles an hour. I crouched down in a fetal position and covered myself with a blanket. I waited until we left the parking lot to sit up. I turned around and sighed with relief as they got further away. Grandpa snickered and exclaimed, "What are you so scared of?" I froze. Grandma put her hand on his shoulder and broke the silence. "That couple behind us thought Joey was staring at them, but he didn't know better. That part wasn't his fault. I'll handle things with them on Wednesday. It'll be all right, dear." He shrugged and said, "Just tell them to mind their business. Joey can look wherever he wants to. What's so scary about that?" She smiled back and replied, "Nothing, dear. I said I'd handle it. How about we go to Braum's for ice cream?" He raised his hand and quietly uttered, "No." I mumbled, "Are you sure, Grandpa? Ice cream doesn't sound good to you?" He cut me off and yelled, "Just drop it!" I covered my nose and mouth to hide my rapid breathing. We all stayed silent for the rest of the car ride. He packed up the Blazer and left for the truck stop. We both watched him drive out from the kitchen window. Grandma said, "I'll talk to those people at the church on Wednesday, just like I said. In the future, I need you to do me a favor. It's one thing to call out people's behavior in a calm and diplomatic way. There's nothing wrong with that if they're actually being unreasonable. This does not mean you should insult them. Calling that guy a hypocrite is where you went wrong, capeesh?" I nodded along and returned to my room. We went on as if nothing happened.

Grandma drove me back to the church for religious education class on Wednesday. It was in a separate building next to the main church. In some ways, it reminded me of an old-time school building from a Western movie. There was vintage-style wood paneling and bricks on the walls. It seemed as if John Wayne might appear at any second. I took a seat in one of the wooden chairs. I wanted to know the why behind everything. I wanted straightforward answers that I could understand. I bluntly asked the hard questions and didn't mince words. This made a lot of people uncomfortable. Everyone seemed leery of what I would say next.

One of the biggest virtues we were taught was that lying is wrong. We were taught that we should always tell the truth, no matter what. That was easy for me to understand. It made sense. Honesty was the best policy, right? Unbeknownst to me, there were instances where it was not socially acceptable to tell the raw truth. People often asked questions that were not really questions at all.

One of the moms looked at me and said, "Aren't my kids the most adorable thing you've ever seen?" I pointed at one and said, "Well, not him. He keeps calling me names and taking my stuff. He acts like an annoying brat with no discipline! What is adorable about that?" Her eyes got narrow. "Excuse me?" I shrugged my shoulders in response. "You asked me a question, and I gave you the truth. We just talked about how lying is wrong, so I'm doing the right thing. Did you want me to lie to you?" Her mouth hung open as her eyes opened wide. She looked at my Grandma in disbelief.

Grandma smiled, waved, and walked to the car. Nothing seemed out of the ordinary. I followed behind. She slammed the car door and looked back at me. She could see that I was clueless, which only fueled the fire. She shook her head and got more furious each second. With little warning, she screamed out, "You CAN NOT say that!" It scared me so bad that I got my breath knocked out of me. I put my hand on my chest and felt it thumping wildly. I was breathing hard. I covered my ears and hunched my back. I had no clue if she was going to scream again. I was scared beyond belief. This outburst came with no warning. Everything was perfectly calm thirty seconds ago. Why was she so angry now?

Grandma saw me covering my ears in the mirror and pressed her lips together. She put her fist to her forehead and closed her eyes. She looked at the cross atop of the church and mumbled,

"Sorry!" She reached back to put her hand on my knee and comfort me. I didn't know what she was doing. I flinched. She couldn't hold back the tears any longer. "Okay, okay, I'm sorry! Please...say something. This silence is killing me." I cleared my throat. "Everything I said in there was true. She lets them do whatever they want. She never gets onto them, even when they are picking on me. That's what I meant when I said they have no discipline. She asked, and I told her the truth!" Grandma replied, "Yeah, well, that may be true, but you still can't say it. There are rules of etiquette everyone needs to follow. Just because you were taught to be honest doesn't mean you get to insult people." I was so confused. After a long car ride of arguing and fussing, I couldn't take it anymore. I came into the kitchen, looked her in the eye, and asked, "Okay, what am I supposed to say? Just tell me what to say next time, and I'll say it!" Grandma started to yell a rebuttal, but she stopped herself. She set her dishrag down and took a deep breath. "I guess...I don't know. You just can't say that. People get their feelings hurt too easily." With tears in my eyes, I looked back up at her and mumbled, "How was I supposed to know that? I have no idea what will or won't hurt feelings. Everything I said was true! You said that you wanted me to start taking up for myself. I'm starting to wonder if you really meant that. I told the truth...and look where it got me!"

Incidents like this started piling up over time. I often got in trouble for reasons I did not understand at all. I became known as the kid who was "difficult." People's faces lit up when Grandma walked in, but not so much with me. I was falling behind; I could feel it in my gut. People were starting to notice my lagging social abilities. The gap was getting bigger. When the social problems started, I felt helpless. I didn't know what to say back to people. They always had a generous supply of comebacks. Everyone had a superpower that I didn't. I was no longer a normal kid by my peers' standards. What they called "normal" was not normal to me at all. I didn't really know how I was supposed to act or what the right thing to say was.

Friday night at Dr. Mac's office, we sat in the lobby like always. I stayed quiet and waited for the sun to go down. I could practically smell Long John Silver's already. Our turn came. I went back to the office. We usually talked about behavior or academics, but we started differently this time. "There is something we haven't discussed in a while. What kind of relationship do you think you have with your peers right now? We haven't addressed this in a little bit, and I thought we should revisit it. Your grandmother had some slight concerns when we talked."

I was taken aback by the question. It came out of nowhere. I raised my eyebrows and rolled with it. "Well, I have two really good friends that I can trust. I spend pretty much every second of the day I can with them. Things are okay most of the time with my grandparents, but when they're not around, it tends to get rough. People are treating me like I'm different. The problem is that I'm not the one who changed; they did. I'm starting to notice this, especially at church for some reason."

The doc nodded his head and said, "What kind of 'different' are we talking about here?" "...Well, people are starting to talk to me in a snarky voice, so I think you can do the math. The weird part is they have never treated me like this before. Until now, they were always nice to me, like I was one of their friends. They all turned mean so suddenly, and I just don't get it. I don't know what caused them to change their attitude. There is no way to please everyone, no matter how hard I try. I can never live up to

45

their expectations. They watch me like they're just waiting for me to mess up. What I do is never good enough for them."

The doc could tell that he was onto something. He asked, "Would you say that you are starting to care what people think of you? Does it cross your mind often?" I shrugged my shoulders. "I don't have much choice. What they think of me directly affects how I am treated. I don't know what I'm doing wrong, though! That's the frustrating part. Why do people have to take everything so personally? When someone told me I should brush my teeth so that my breath doesn't stink, I didn't take that personally; I just did it because it made sense! When I call out other people's behavior, they get all mean and defensive, like I'm attacking them as a person. Why is that? Why can't everybody just listen to logic and give a logical response? Why does there have to be confusing emotional signals behind everything?"

He chuckled and nodded. He said, "You know what? You might have a point there. Life would be a whole lot simpler that way, wouldn't it? That's one of those subtle differences between an autistic way of thinking and the way the outside world thinks. When you said that the gentleman at church was being hypocritical, he probably took that as you calling him a person with low integrity." I snapped back, "Whoa, I never said a word about his integrity! I only said that his *words* were hypocritical, not the whole person! That means he said two things that contradicted each other, and it made no logical sense. I just wanted clarification."

The doc continued, "Exactly. You saw it in the logical sense, but there is a negative association behind words like 'hypocrite' and other terms that address a person's behavior. Your words had consequences that you didn't intend or even know about.

I Have a Reason

Remember that gap between your social patterns and your peers' patterns that we discussed a while back? Well, unfortunately, that gap is starting to grow. It will get better eventually, but it may get worse before it gets better..." He kept talking, but I had already zoned out.

Wednesday night, my religious education class headed to the church for a service. I tripped on a rug. When I did, one of my toy airplanes fell out of my coat pocket. I bent down to pick it up, only to see that everyone was staring at me. I mumbled, "What?" The teacher's heels clicked my way. She crouched down to eye level. She held her hand out and whispered, "Here, I can hold onto it for you. I'll keep it safe. I promise. Can you please hand it over?" She slowly leaned closer. I got claustrophobic and backed up. My head felt like it was about to explode. I panicked and started talking fast. "No, no! I need it! It keeps me calm. You don't get it. You're not like me. You don't have ADHD or autism, for that matter." One of my classmates fixed her hair as she was exasperated. She looked back and said, "Why can't you just be normal for once?" Two others giggled when she said this. They covered their mouths to hide it. Something about that rubbed me the wrong way. I usually tried to avoid confrontation, but I lost it this time. I shouted, "What do you mean, 'normal?' Do you want to come over here and explain yourself?"

The teacher shook her head and motioned for me to turn around and go back. I stepped forward and said, "I want to know what she meant by that. Where I come from, if you can say something behind a person's back, then you should have got the guts to say it to their face! Why doesn't she come over here and say it again?" The teacher held me back and said, "Because that's not how this works. Now back you go. Yep, you know where the office is. It's the last door on the right." I slouched down the sidewalk to the school building. A cross was reflected in the door glass. I looked straight at it and said, "You are not fair! None of this is fair."

My frustration gradually turned into resentment. Grandma had to drag me to church from this day forward. I cannot count the times she grabbed my ear and said, "One hour a week for God won't kill you!" It always felt like more than that. Time seemed to go slower on Sundays and Wednesdays. There was always a fight to get me out the door in time. Once we were there, the arguing continued. If I ranted in front of other people, she said, "Do you want to be here all day? If so, go ahead and keep complaining!" She started hanging out longer on purpose to make a point. Our car was one of the last cars to leave the parking lot. The more time I spent at church, the more I hated it.

I always thought church was supposed to be a place of acceptance, but I felt none of that. I was in a big building with hundreds of people, but I somehow felt more alone there than anywhere else in the world. Everyone pointed out my flaws and how different I was from the other kids. My circumstances were not changing. The treatment was getting worse. During the car ride home, I spoke up. "Grandma, if God is truly all-powerful, then why won't He do anything about my autism? Why is He allowing me to get treated like this? Is it all just a big joke to Him? I don't get it." She gripped the steering wheel tight and looked at the horizon. "What you need to remember is that most kids don't understand autism. The majority of parents don't have a clue either. That part is on them, not you. Many people are uptight and judgmental toward anyone who isn't exactly like them. That is not right, but they still do it. I don't like this any more than you do."

I interlocked my fingers in my hair. "Hold on a second. You're telling me that I will never be normal? Not even for one day? This is how my entire life is going to be? Why me? Why can't my autism be transferred to an evil person who deserves to live like this?" It was just as painful for her to hear as it was for me to say.

I had no clue that this was the battle that awaited me. Everything changed when I became old enough to care what people thought of me. My eyes were opened, and I could never un-see it. I wasn't finding the acceptance I wanted at church, so I would have to find it somewhere else.

CHAPTER SEVEN — Just a Big Misunderstanding

"Go ahead and smile," the photographer said. I narrowed my eyes and clammed up. I pretended to scratch my ear so I could cover it. Despite my efforts, I still jumped a little. Jeez, that camera click was loud! Nobody else thought so, just me. I acted like I was sick that morning, but Grandma wasn't buying it. So, there I was: the third kid in line at the library. It was school picture day.

Everyone stepped forward. Now there was only one kid standing between me and that terrifying death machine. At least I was the last one in line. That gave me some comfort, but not much. I looked up at a fly buzzing on the ceiling and was nearly blinded. This time, I flinched for real. The photographer adjusted his lens and grunted, "Next!" It was my turn to go to the chopping block. I did not know how to smile for pictures. The noise and flash always scared me. This is why I looked like a pterodactyl in some of my yearbook photos.

I moseyed to the chair and sat down. "All right, look into this black box right here." The veins popped out of my neck. I tried to keep my eyes open and not jump out of the chair. "Three, two, one!" There was an awkward pause after the flash. "Let's try that again. You look a little tense." A big group of kids walked in. "Great..."

The photographer pressed buttons for several seconds. He got ready to take another one. My neck and cheeks got tougher than a leather boot. I was lucky to keep my mouth open at all. It snapped again, and the second picture was no better than the first. I shook my head and looked at the door. The photographer exclaimed, "Hold on, son, let's try one last time before you take off." My heart was racing a thousand miles an hour. My eyes were darting all over the place. I held the best smile I could make and desperately whispered, "Please get this over with!" The flash made me jump again. The other kids started giggling. I couldn't stand this anymore. I made a beeline for the door. "Sir, we're not done here." I just ran faster and turned away. "I don't care! You people are so immature!"

I sat in the back of the classroom when I returned. I liked to sit there because nobody could see me stimming. Stimming was a side effect of my autism. In the medical community, it refers to repetitive behaviors, gestures, or sounds. One of these is spinning hands or arms. It is a way to release energy, cope with anxiety, or distract from overwhelming situations. The urge to stim came to me during high anxiety moments. The sensation had many similarities to a yawn. I'm talking about one of the good ones: The type of yawn where the eyes close and the mouth naturally wants to open as wide as the Grand Canyon. My body set itself up to stim, and I went along with it. It was very unpredictable but, like yawning, it was not uncontrollable. I could hide it if I really wanted to, but it made anxiety harder to deal with. All of that ADHD energy had to go somewhere.

The whole class went for a bathroom break and formed a line. I was in the back as always. People returned to class, and I accidentally slipped up. I allowed myself to make a spinning motion with my hands in front of the wrong person. A sarcastic voice yelled, "What are you trying to do there, buddy? Are you trying to reenact the school bus going round and round song?" He spun his arms to mock me. His friends quickly followed suit and laughed. I buried my face in my hoodie, but it didn't do any good. There was nowhere to hide. This was humiliation like I had never experienced before. I couldn't take it; I had to run away. I went back to class and waited for the rest to return. From this moment forward, the guys tried to time it right and copy me. They made childish bus noises as they mimicked me. They made faces like a mother does when they play with a baby. I wanted to knock those guys' teeth into the stratosphere. Words have not been invented yet to describe just how badly I wanted to. I knew I couldn't, though.

The teacher waltzed in and said, "All right guys, last chance. Nobody needs to make a pit stop before we start the lesson?" I opened my mouth, but no words came out. The pressure was paralyzing. She shrugged and shut the door. I pushed my desk as far back as I could. An hour passed, and I began struggling internally. I had to decide which one I was more afraid of: soiling my pants or speaking up. My face got red as I clenched my fist. I had to think fast. One girl chuckled and whispered, "Joey, what are you doing?" I raised my hand. The teacher rolled her eyes and pointed at the hall pass hanging on the chalkboard. "Next time, you better take care of that when everyone else does." I busted out the door. I was so scared that I wouldn't make it to the bathroom in time. I barely did by the skin of my teeth. I shrugged it off and tried to forget about all this.

The next morning, Grandpa was at the table eating his pancakes. He said, "...Just so you know, you are more mature than most kids your age. I hope you remember that." That was highly debatable, but I did appreciate where his heart was. At recess, I found my group and continued the game of tag where we left off the day prior.

Ten or more guys approached the playground like paparazzi. Their mischievous grins were as wide as the sky. They looked at my friends and yelled, "Hey, you! Come here! We've got a question for you!" One of them looked at me and crossed his arms. He had every right to be skeptical. "Are you too chicken? Get over here!" They made clucking noises and flapped their arms. They knew this would tick him off. He lost his temper and stormed over. "What do you want?" They mocked his voice and kept clucking. The leader of the group said, "Easy there, big boy! We just have one question. Are you gay?" They all smiled and waited for him to answer. He hesitantly replied, "What does that mean?" We were deer in the headlights. We had no clue, and the bullies took advantage of that. They said, "It just means you're happy! That's all!" They started giggling wildly.

They waved the rest of their group to come over. They huddled in and crowded us. "So, are you and Joey gay?" I swiped my hand and shook my head. I was hoping my friends would get the hint and keep their mouths shut. Unfortunately, they didn't understand my signal. The mob wore us down and tricked us. "All right... fine. Do you like hotdogs, big man?" Without thinking, one of my friends blurted out, "Yeah, sure, they're all right. What does that have to do with this? I don't get it." Everyone smiled and jumped up and down with glee. They got happier than a dog with a bone. "Did y'all hear that? He just admitted he's gay! That's nasty, man! We better get away from him! If he touches you, you will catch the gayness!" Everyone ran away laughing.

We didn't understand why they were laughing, but we knew it wasn't good. My friend sighed and said, "I just messed up, didn't I?" My nose scrunched as I began breathing hard. "When someone swipes their hand over their neck, that is a signal to keep your dang mouth shut! I tried to save you from the embarrassment, but you blatantly ignored me! Why did you keep going when they started laughing?" He looked down at the ground. "I'm sorry...I didn't know that! I had no idea what you were trying to do. When those people crowded me, I panicked. I really thought I could fix this!" He glanced up at the empty playground house. He kicked up sand with his shoe. "What does that word mean anyway? Why was it so funny to them?" "I have no idea. I'll try to handle this before it gets out of hand."

I found a teacher, and we all told her what was happening. She shrugged her shoulders and said, "One of us didn't see it, so we can't prove anything yet. I'll keep an eye out. Just ignore them! If they don't get a rise out of you, they'll get bored and leave." She smiled like life was just that simple. I did the best I could to hide my frustration. "So, you're essentially saying that I should let them walk all over me?" She crouched down and said, "I'm on your side, but the important thing is that you can't rock the boat. If you provoke a fight, that violates our zero-tolerance policy. You would be suspended. Do you really want that?" She stood back up and pulled her sunglasses. "Go play with your other friends. What are you guys doing over here when they're all over there?" "Those people are *not* our friends! Thanks for nothing."

That was one long week. Gossip was a powerful force at my small-town school. Every day was worse than the last. It started out as innocent giggles when my friends or I walked into a room. Later on, it escalated. Several feet clobbered the tile floor as I walked in from recess one day. Naturally, I turned around to find the source. The biggest kid in the group yelled, "What are you looking at?" I knew it was Braxton before I ever saw him. He always wore chain wallets, chain necklaces, and chain bracelets. That sound was unmistakable. He typically wore jeans with skulls printed on them. He came around the corner and charged at me for the fun of it. He got three inches away from my face. The duct tape holding his shoes together crinkled. He looked up at me through his brows. Sweat was dripping off his nose. Every time he breathed, it splashed onto me. My bottom jaw tingled.

My voice was shaking as I said, "What do you want, Braxton?" His friends smiled and started whispering to each other. He punched a locker to make me flinch. His fists were calloused. Word on the street was that Braxton had been in several fights. I backed up, but they just kept coming. "If you're going to be a fag, then we're just going to have to treat you like it!" They cracked their knuckles. My heart pounded so hard that my temples were pulsating. I looked around for an adult, but there was nobody to be seen. My breaths got faster and lighter. "...Aww, you're not going to cry, are you? Everyone knows a real man doesn't cry! You're a bigger gay-wad than we thought!" I got so scared that my bottom jaw tingled. I could barely speak. "Wait, they told us that word meant, 'happy.' Does it mean something else?" They laughed hysterically. One guy jabbed his finger in my face. "Duh, idiot, it's you! You should know what it means because you're disgusting!" He wiped his hands as if they were exposed to something dirty. They all left just as fast as they came.

I went home that day and saw a bucket on the kitchen floor. Water was slowly dripping into it from the ceiling. The A/C wasn't running. "Hey, Grandma, what does gay mean? A bunch of people keep calling me that, and I have no idea why." She froze in disbelief for a second. Finally, someone explained it to me. "Well, that is when two guys kiss each other…" I couldn't hold the tears in any longer. "WHAT? That is what they are accusing me of? I have never kissed anybody and don't want to…I'm ten years old! What is wrong with those people? Can we please move somewhere else? I want to go to another school district." Her nose scrunched. She picked up the phone and nearly breathed out fire as she dialed. "What's the little scumbag's name who said that to you? I can track down that kid's parents and settle this the old-fashioned way! I can get my hands dirty. My daddy didn't raise a chicken! No sir! You just watch me!" I panicked when I heard the dial tone. "Please wait! Stop, you don't know the full story!" I unplugged the answering machine to stop the call. She crossed her arms and said, "This better be good."

"It is not just one kid. It is a big group of them acting together. My friends are under fire for the exact same thing. The group started the rumor, and it is out of control. There is no stopping it. I already talked to a teacher, and they wouldn't do anything. She said they don't have enough proof. Those guys will retaliate if they find out I snitched! This could get really bad. Please don't tell the principal. Just get me out of there!"

She sighed and bowed her head. "Your grandfather left Hobby Lobby to become an owner-operator. The money was supposed to be better. He does make more, but he spends more too. Just the self-employment tax and trucking fees alone are eating us alive! Something is always going out on the truck. I tried to tell him that leaving Hobby Lobby was the dumbest thing he could ever do! He's definitely bringing home less than before. Now, of course, the home A/C went out again. We're going to have to pay for that, too! I guess that's what I get for owning a hundred-year-old house. Sorry to say this, but we're not moving or doing a whole lot of anything for a while. I can't drive you because I have to be at work in the city at 7:40. I guess I could transfer you to the city with me, but you'd have to stay for all of my meetings. Well, actually, my school has a bunch of problems in it too. The parents don't even care if their children behave up there! I think where you are is your best bet. Plug the phone back up. Someone needs to pay dearly. I want you to grab that yearbook over there and tell me every single one of the names that started this mess. I'm going to teach those school administrators a lesson. They will never forget this call!" I finally told her the full story. She got more furious with each detail. I told her as much as I could before I started falling asleep. It was really late. I finally called it a night at nine o'clock or so. By the time she picked that phone up, I felt sorry for whoever picked up the other end of that line.

I got off the bus the next day and looked around. Everything was surprisingly peaceful. I had no clue what she said on the phone the night prior, but it must have been an earful. Several teachers had their eyes on me. When we were released for lunch, I was within earshot of the same group who had started the rumor. One of them saw me and slowly clapped his hands. "Hey, you! Just remember, no one likes a snitch. They get stitches! You best watch yourself. Braxton is a scary dude. That's all I'm going to say." He smiled from ear to ear before turning back around. Perhaps he was just messing with me. I had no way to tell.

A teacher started getting on the group's case, but I told her to stop. Confrontation was never what I wanted. I didn't want to start a war with kids who were twice my size. I just wanted to put this rumor behind me and enjoy the last year of elementary school in peace. I didn't want to rely on teachers to get me by. Freedom was my biggest desire of all. I wanted to be free from all of the social barriers that were holding me back. My hope was that I would grow up to be a halfway respected guy. I wanted to live in a world where I never had to worry about bullying again. Unfortunately, that world did not exist for me yet. That was a reality that I couldn't quite have.

I lived a quiet and uneventful life for the rest of elementary school. I hung out with my small group of friends and kept a healthy distance from the problematic kids. I stayed within eyeshot of a teacher at all times. I toed the line and maintained the peace. The whole time, I was suppressing an anxious feeling. I knew that I was putting off the inevitable. Middle school was coming the next year, whether I was ready for it or not. It would be a defining point. I had to choose who I was going to become. One thing was for sure: I needed to start making major changes to my social strategy.

CHAPTER EIGHT — **One Swish at a Time**

I paced around the house at 4:30 in the morning. I was freaking out. Grandma turned on the light and plugged in the coffee maker. "Don't worry, I'll drive you to school today. I have a question about your schedule anyway." We took off just before dawn. We got to town, and I lay down in the seat. "What are you doing?" I put my headphones on and crossed my arms. "I can't be seen in this car! All of the cool kids show up in sports cars or trucks." She shook her head. I sprayed one last bit of Axe down my shirt for good measure. As we pulled into the lot, I asked her to slow down. I opened the door and scurried out. The door slammed behind me. She rolled the window down and yelled, "Gee, love you too, sweetie!" She revved and parked at the office. My eyes were darting everywhere. Did anybody see me? I guess not...good thing.

This was my first year of junior high. A huge crowd gathered on the far side of campus like always. Our bus depot was the main transportation hub for the district. The whole crowd was walking to the same building. The cafeteria and basketball gym were connected to each other. We grabbed our snacks and walked over to the gym. We were seated in sections based on which grade we were in. I could not find my friends. They were at the office getting their schedules changed. I took a seat along the back wall of the bleachers. The brand-new hit song, "Gangnam Style," was blasting over the speakers. The older kids went crazy. Some of the more zealous ones crossed their arms at their wrists. They were mimicking a dance move for which this song was famous. There was enough energy in the stands to travel to the moon and back.

A shadow emerged from the locker room. It was the school basketball team. They ran out one at a time. The first guy ran onto the court and pounded the ball down with a colossal thud. It sounded like a gun blast. The ball flew high in the air. He pumped his fist to his chest and hollered, "Yeah, that's right! That's right! You know what's up!" He raised his hands to hype the crowd. They directed their attention to him and started stomping the bleachers. He caught the ball as the rest of the team joined him on the court. The crowd erupted with applause. They were just about to blow off the roof of this joint. There was no mistaking who the true stars were in that building. All eyes were on them. They started their practice in front of the entire school. Everyone on the bottom rows crowded the railing. They leaned over to get high-fives from the players as they sprinted by.

The first bell rang, and we were released into the wild. The hallways seemed to go on forever. There were exposed pipes and concrete blocks in the ceiling. This was the biggest school I had ever been in. The girls got busy taping Justin Bieber and One Direction posters to their lockers. Their binders were covered with Big Time Rush stickers. Most of the guys wore OKC Thunder hoodies. There was an unspoken currency system. Beef jerky and Pop Tarts could be traded for homework answers, favors, or whatever one's heart desired. Pokémon cards were big too, but I never got into that.

There were cheers coming from the main hallway. Someone ran behind me and pointed at the entrance. "They're here!" The doors exploded open. The basketball team had a mob of paparazzi following them in. Camera flashes bounced off the metal lockers and tile floor. Everywhere these guys went, prestige went with them. Their lives were a non-stop party. A black-and-gold jersey was an all-access pass to royalty. Everyone talked basketball lingo and had the style to back it up. Nike and Jordan were the ultimate status symbols. We had two courts on campus. Basketball was the lifeblood of our school culture. It was everything.

I tried to blend in with the crowd, but I kept getting ignored. They wanted nothing to do with me. This trend continued in class. The girl in front of me leaned back in her chair. She asked, "Why are you so quiet?" I never liked that question because it put me on the spot. I shrugged back and said, "That's just who I am. I'm not sitting here asking why you are so loud, am I? That is such a double standard. Just tell me what you want to talk about." She acted like she didn't hear me. She let her hair down and joined her friends a few desks forward.

I complained about this to my friends in the lunch line. A guy heard me and scooted up. "Do you want to know why people are treating you like that? It's because you're too nice. You always play by the rules. That's your problem, player! If you let those idiotic teachers dictate your life, you will always be a nobody. You've got to be a rebel to win at this game. They play hardball in this school. I want you to remember a phrase. 'Nice guys finish last.' Got it? Don't limit yourself to those bullshit rules!"

I nervously looked around. "Dude, you're going to get in trouble if a teacher hears you!" He smirked and said, "That's the point, junior. I don't give a flying shit what the rules say! I do whatever the hell I want. I say whatever the hell I want. I always stand my ground, and you know what? Nobody messes with me anymore. It's all about confidence, man, confidence. Find out what the popular kids are doing and try to copy that. You'll get there."

I took the cross necklace out of my shirt and fidgeted with it. He rolled his eyes and said, "Oh wait! Now I get it. It's that stupid thing around your neck! That is just a bunch of fairytales made to control you. Those rules are made for losers by losers. That's all that is, Joey! Let me guess. They treat you like an outcast at your church, too, don't they?" I raised my eyebrows with surprise. "Hey, how the heck did you know that?" He shook his head and smiled. "Oh, I could just tell. Those people don't even practice what they preach!" He pointed at the necklace. "My advice is to let go of that fairytale. All of these years, you've been toeing the line, and you have nothing to show for it. If God is so real, why do bad people always win in life? Nothing ends well for the good guys like you. Think about it! The bad boy gets the girl, the promotion, and the big money. Nobody in the sky is coming to change that. The movies have been lying to you. People make their own luck. One day you'll grow a pair and realize I'm right. Best of luck, player."

We ate in the cafeteria, and I thought about what he said. It got in my head and messed with my outlook. I had been frustrated with church and the status quo for a long time. I was tired of following rules that benefited everyone but me. It seemed as though the entire system of social etiquette was rigged against me. What if that guy was right the whole time? Perhaps my compliance was the only barrier that stood between me and a better life. I was sick and tired of being a charity case. I wanted to stand on my own two feet. I decided, as of this day, no more Mr. Nice guy! I tossed my tray in the pile and went behind the gym. I ripped the necklace off and chunked it in the dumpster. I gave up on God and everything I was raised to believe in. I got out of speech therapy and quit going to the psychologist. I didn't need them any longer. It was time to do things my way for a change.

When class started one day, the intercom speaker came on, and everyone paused to listen to the daily announcements. "Our basketball coaches are now recruiting players! It's time to expand the team for the new season. If you are interested in signing up, please come to the attendance office after the bell rings. Best of luck, guys!" I saw a basketball hoodie stuffed in a chair at the front of the classroom. I stared intently at it for the whole class hour. I got goosebumps. I suddenly wanted one of those more than anything in the world. I wanted to become a basketball player, just like the popular kids. That would change my whole life. People would finally respect me again! I knew exactly what I needed to do.

I couldn't wait for class to end. I watched the clock so I would be ready to bolt. Several others had the same idea. The line was horrendously long. The tardy bell rang, and I missed my chance. The classroom door was shut, which meant I had to go back for a tardy slip. I had no problem returning to the office. The lady behind the desk was talking to someone in a suit. I had no business interrupting, but I had to try. I mustered the courage to speak up. "Do you have any sign-up sheets for basketball?" She shook her head and shrugged her shoulders. She licked her thumb and went back to sorting her stack of papers. I assumed the answer was no. I started to leave. As I turned the corner, she spoke up. "Well, actually, I have one left. Are you really serious about this?" I perked up and sprinted back. "Yes, ma'am." She smiled and pushed the door buzzer. "Come on in and take it. Best of luck to you. I hope you make the cut."

Maybe I had a sliver of hope, after all. Now I needed to get accepted onto the team. It was my best chance to escape bullying for good. If I made a name for myself in basketball, I could ride that wave to the top. This would allow me to completely surpass my enemies and leave them in the dust. It seemed like a solid plan to me. No one would mess with a popular guy who had connections. I didn't view it as trying out for a sports team. I saw a chance for a better life. I wanted to be somebody.

I filled out the form in my best handwriting. Grandpa told me how important first impressions were. I was careful not to fold or crease the paper. I waited until the end of the day to turn it in, so my name would be near the top of the stack. This was everything to me; I needed it to work out. I barely slept or ate while I waited for news. I lost several pounds during those two weeks. This wasn't intentional on my part. I didn't want to stop what I was doing to eat. I worked on muscle building like my life depended on it. My fingernails were almost chewed down to nothing. Monday would be my moment of truth.

I raced through the cafeteria, straight to the bulletin board in the hallway. The team lineups were pinned to the board. The list was long. The pages were stapled together. At the very back, my name was there. I was officially a basketball player. Time seemed to stand still. My skin tingled. There was no one around to hug, so I held my stack of books to my chest as tightly as I could. I hadn't been this happy in a long, long time.

The intercom speaker came on. "Joey Perry, please report to the gym." I pressed my lips together to hide my dorky smile. I almost got happy tears. I couldn't believe this was really happening. I raced down to the coach's office to pick up my team merchandise. I got the same gray hoodie and sweatpants that the other recruits had. They were made of a soft, athletic fabric. I also got a team backpack with brand-new Nike Airs. There was a special pocket to hold the basketball shoes. My name was embroidered on the bag in golden yellow. I couldn't wait for my life to start changing.

I knew nothing about basketball. I did not understand the plays and code words or how to shoot the ball. I didn't even have a genuine passion for the sport yet. The real work started after the crowd left for class. I spent so many hours on the court that I learned to like it. The exercise was good for me. I spent a lot of time on the bench press. I pushed myself to the limit. I used it as an outlet for all of that pent-up frustration. My anger became my motivation. I left the court soaked with sweat but relieved. It was my own version of therapy.

I got in the best shape of my life. Working out did wonders for my confidence. Before I knew it, I was one of the top benchers on the team. I found a sense of pride that I didn't know I had. Someone challenged me to arm wrestle, and I won in seconds. "Hold up, dog! Let me get a crack at it!" Another guy sat down, and another one lost. Then another and another. There was a long stretch of time where I remained undefeated. I became known as the "arm wrestling king." It was our inside joke as a team. Between you and me, that was just luck. At least I was accepted by my peers for something. It gave me something to talk about.

I walked into the cafeteria for lunch. Someone yelled, "Hey, hey! This is Joey's spot now, dog!" The team looked at me and pounded the table for a drumroll entrance. I looked at my reflection in the window and saw something strange. Was I actually...smiling? I shook my head in disbelief. I mumbled to myself, "I can get used to this!" and strutted to the table as if I owned the place.

Braxton, my long-time nemesis, approached the table. He said, "Just who do you think you are, bigshot? You think you're somebody important now?" He smirked and crossed his arms. My teammates gave him heck for it. "He's one of us now, that's who he is! If you have a problem with him, then that is a problem for us too. I don't think you want that." The room got quiet. I couldn't believe it, but Braxton cowered down. He rolled his eyes and tried to play it off. "Gee, sorry, bro, I was just messing with him! We're guys, we do that!" I waved and gave him a big fat smile. I said, "It was nice knowing you." He stood there with his hands on his hips. Another teammate got up and pointed at the door. "You heard the man, it's time for you to leave." The room held eye contact with him. Braxton shook his head with embarrassment. Everybody laughed as he stormed off. From this day forward, he kept a healthy distance from me.

People started coming out of the woodwork, one by one. The same guys who started the rumor about me in elementary school were suddenly nice. The group found me in the hallway and approached. They patted me on the back and said nice things to butter me up. One guy hugged my neck before telling me, "All of that stuff we said to you before was just a big misunderstanding. We didn't mean any of that, man! It was all Braxton's fault. That guy sucks; we're done with him. We're on your side, JP! Remember that when you get popular." For the first time, I held all the cards. Boy, how the tables had turned. My ego ate this up.

I was beyond stoked for Tuesday night. I put on a Number 52 jersey for my first home game. They called my name over the speakers, and I raced out of the locker room. The student section went crazy, and so did the other players. There were camera flashes everywhere. I was so happy to be playing in front of my peers in that gym. I enjoyed every second of the spotlight that I could. I never knew it could feel so good.

Later on, we had a couple of away games. The schoolyard fence was decorated with streamers in preparation. People pushed Styrofoam cups into the pores of the fence to spell out our team's name. Everyone wore black and gold all week long. On the big day, our coach pulled up the bus and rolled the windows down. Maroon 5 was blasting over the speakers. A bunch of people wanted me to take pictures with them before I left. The coach motioned for me to hurry up, so I kept going. Our peers crowded the bus and chanted as we rolled out of the lot. Car horns were honking. My teammates were sticking their hands out the window and slapping the roof. I followed suit. People ran across the field and crowded the fence. They climbed on each other's backs to get a better view. One girl climbed up a tree branch. She screamed at the top of her lungs, "This is it! The tournaments are here!" She ripped up one of the streamers and threw it like confetti. Everyone rattled the fence as we left town.

I smiled and thought to myself, "Finally! I have made it!" My plan was working out beautifully. Joining basketball seemed like the greatest decision I had ever made. I felt good about myself again. I had officially won my dignity back. Life was never better.

CHAPTER NINE — Friends and Foes

The bus pulled up in the morning, and I decided to swing by the cafeteria. I hadn't taken a victory lap in a while. Somebody was getting picked on, and I happened to see it. Three or four people were going after one guy. They all had their backs turned to me. Someone yelled, "This dude is definitely a wimp. I mean, look at those praying mantis arms!" They cracked with laughter. One of them saw my reflection in the glass and turned around. They beamed with glee. "Hey, there's JP! Now that is what a stud looks like right there. You ladies better control yourselves! Flex your arms, Joey! Show this loser what real muscles look like." I smirked and played along. They clapped with admiration. One of them slapped my bicep and whispered, "Don't you agree that guy is a wimp over there? Say it, say it!" I paused and felt conflicted. I didn't want to participate in this. The guy rolled his eyes and grunted in frustration. "Come on now, JP! Don't hang me out to dry! I know you're cooler than that. Embrace the dark side, brother. That's the thing about being popular; you don't have to be nice anymore!" He spun his hand to push me to respond. I gave into the pressure and did what was popular. I smirked and said, "You're totally right! That dude has got some serious work to do. He's skinny enough to be thrown like a football!" The whole table exploded with laughter. I did not expect my words to get such a big reaction. The bully hugged my neck and yelled, "That's our boy! He's already acting like a boss.

I love it, man, you're a natural!" I walked down the stairs to the locker room. I felt icky inside. I hated that I caved in and bullied someone that easily. I realized that I would do just about anything for praise.

I got my basketball gear on and did my usual. I rotated around the court baskets and tried to make them all. I didn't make any fuss. One of my teammates pulled me aside. He said, "Man, what a buzzkill. You are a basketball player. You know what that means? A freaking superstar! Start acting like it! If you want the crowd to cheer for you, give them something to cheer for! Get cocky out there. They love it when you give them some attitude." I shrugged my shoulders and replied, "Well, I don't want to make an ass of myself. I'm not arrogant like that." He rolled his eyes and said, "Who cares? Just act like you are. Don't hold yourself back. Release your inner jackass! They adore that kind of confidence." He pulled my sunglasses down and pressed them on my face. "Try it, man. You'll see!" As he said this, the music came on over the speakers.

I smirked and decided to roll with it. I picked the basketball back up and ran out to the middle. I waited for the beat of the song to drop and pounded the ball down with all my might. I flexed my arms and yelled like a gladiator. "We're in the house! Let's hear it, y'all! This is getting pretty sad!" I caught the basketball and held it over my head like a trophy. The team started chanting my name and howling like a bunch of college frat boys. Some people in the bottom rows nodded their heads and joined the chant. They stomped the bleachers so hard I thought it was an earthquake. The chant migrated up the bleachers and got louder. Their energy buzzed through my veins. I loved every second of it.

I never wanted this feeling to stop! I felt like the king of the world. The addiction was instantaneous.

I smiled back at my teammate and chucked the ball at him. I exclaimed, "Get your ass out here! You're missing all the fun!" He hugged my neck and messed up my hair. He whispered, "Now you're getting it! It feels great, right? Welcome to royalty, JP!"

He patted me on the back and waltzed up to the railing. A group of girls were snapping pictures and trying to get high-fives from him. He motioned for me to join him. He said, "Y'all listen up! This guy is one of us now. I want you ladies to take real good care of him. You know what I'm saying? We need him on his A-game out here!" He pointed back at the court and winked at one of the girls. He uttered, "Just keep his eyes on the prize, okay?"

I smiled and went along with it, but I did not like how that sounded. When we left practice, I talked to him. "Hey, listen. I appreciate the advice, but I don't really want a girlfriend right now." He rolled his eyes and yelled, "Girlfriend? No way, bro! We don't need you getting distracted! You're about to reach the top of your game!" I was so confused by this. "Then what were you doing back there? You said, 'Take care of him' like you were trying to set me up. That's why I'm saying I don't really want that." He exploded with laughter. "Slow your roll! I would tread lightly there if I were you. Those girls have a LOT of power! They control what happens here, especially with the upperclassmen. If they like you, the whole school will. When they start talking you up, you'll be just like me. It is magic, my friend. You can thank me later."

Sure enough, all of that paid off. Nobody messed with me anymore, quite the opposite. My autism no longer affected the way I was treated. For the first time in my life, I was a big deal. A crowd formed everywhere I went. I never had to worry about sitting alone; doing so was nearly impossible. My voice became influential in the crowds. Younger kids started addressing me by my full name like I was a celebrity. A group of them approached me in the bus depot. They asked me to sign their casts and binder covers. Their eyes sparkled as they looked up at me. One of them asked, "What's it like to be famous?" Initially, I tried to laugh it off. I replied, "Hey, slow down! Let's not go that far. That is a level of responsibility that I don't really want." The kid shrugged back, "Do you know who I am?" I awkwardly replied, "Sorry, I don't." He held up his binder and pointed at my signature. He exclaimed, "Well, everybody knows your name! What do you call that?" I smirked and turned around to autograph the next binder.

So many people treated me like this that it went straight to my head. I became full of myself by the end of the season. I was more than confident; I was cocky. I upgraded to a pair of matte-black sunglasses that were tinted red. I let my hair grow long so that it would stick out of my backward hat. If a shirt didn't have the Nike swoosh on it, I didn't want it! I rolled the sleeves up to my forearms. I had a whole new identity. I strutted my weight around left and right. I said whatever the heck I wanted to. I had no fear of anybody. Everyone knew when I walked into the room because I was usually the loudest one.

My arrogance began as an innocent persona that I played while I was on the court. I flipped the switch back off when I left the gym. Little by little, that line got blurry. I learned that the more obnoxious I was, the more praise I got. I pushed the ethical boundaries every day to give the school something to talk about. I didn't want them to forget about me. I had to keep being the latest headline. Being a snake was a whole lot better than being a "nobody." Cursing at teachers and being sarcastic was enough to give me a thrill in the beginning. However, after I did it a few times, the high wore off. Those things didn't excite me anymore. It wasn't bold and daring enough. I had to do crazier and wilder things to get that same rush of excitement.

The teachers were not very fond of the new me. I carried those office write-up sheets with pride. When I walked the hall with a yellow slip in my hand, at least one person would smile and say, "Dude! What the heck did you pull this time?" I bragged to them about what I did with no shame. They would stick their hand out for a fist bump and say, "Nice! That's sick, man! You're crazy!" Their eyes would beam with adoration the whole time. I liked playing the role of the black hat. No one knew what I would try next, including me. It was impulsive half the time. If the day was getting boring, I knew how to spice things up. I wasn't nice on the way up because I thought I would never come back down.

I strutted to class one afternoon and shoved several people out of my way. A girl was sitting alone in the back of the room. She was wearing a dirty old work jacket. Her jeans had holes in them. Her bag was falling apart. She saw me pushing someone's stuff away from the desk I wanted. I sat down and put my feet up. The girl yelled from the back, "Why do you always have to be a jerk?" I laughed and proclaimed, "Oh, just to piss you off! If you get mad enough, smoke will come out of your ears. This is fun, keep going!" She stuck her middle finger up and flipped me off. I smiled and shook my head. I said, "Oh, you sure wish that would happen, don't you? I'm sorry, but I'd have to be high on drugs to sleep with you." The whole room burst into hardy laughter. Some of the guys started clapping and wooing with admiration. They nodded their heads and smiled at me. The girl flipped me off with the other hand. I yelled, "Okay, now you're just being unrealistic! You really think two guys would sleep with you at the same time? You need a drug test!" At this point, the class was dying with laughter. Someone shook my collar and yelled, "We better get the damn fire department in here! Someone's getting burned bad!" I was practically rolling on the floor, just like the rest of them.

When I opened my mouth, I knew I wasn't making the right choice. I thought I would feel guilt and regret. As I kept talking, something strange happened. I started looking around at my peers' reactions. I realized that I was enjoying it much more than I thought I would. All of those claps and smiles became my energy source at that moment. That buzz led me to keep going. I got meaner and meaner. The whole time, I kept thinking to myself, "Why don't I feel guilty about this? This shouldn't feel good, so why does it? This is not me! How do I go back?" My arrogance was no longer an act.

I went to my long-time friends to brag, but they did not react as I expected. They refused to treat me like a superstar the way everyone else did. They were not proud in the slightest. They called me out on my behavior. I rolled my eyes every time. I got frustrated and left. There were many somber faces when I walked into class. They pulled up chairs and whispered, "Why are you still hanging with Andrew and them? They are such a buzzkill. You should ditch them and hang with us!" I tried to defend, but I was too outnumbered. "Ah, give them a chance! They just don't understand how middle school works yet. Everyone makes mistakes. They'll learn." The guys rolled their eyes and laughed at me for trying. "Yeah, well, they make A LOT of mistakes, dude. Do you really want to hang out with people who weigh you down?"

I didn't know how to reply. They all chuckled and patted me on the back as they returned to their seats. They said, "When you're ready to join our table, you know where to find us. Don't bring those liabilities with you. You may think you're balling now, but you have no clue. It's not even funny, bro. You can become more popular than you have ever been before!"

What I did next is one of my biggest regrets. I went to their table in the cafeteria and said that I was in. I bought the lie that my old friends were weak links in my social ecosystem. I believed I was too good for them anymore. I started acting differently when certain people walked by. I talked in a deeper voice and acted like someone I wasn't. I became a stuck-up, pretentious person. I began excluding my old friends and this slowly escalated with time. I told lies about one of them because I wanted him gone for the sake of my reputation. The truth is that he wasn't harassing girls. That was a lie that, I regret to say, I started. I told the rest of the guys that they should distance themselves from him. They briefly obliged. I wish I could say that was my low point, but it wasn't. I got ticked off over someone owing me two dollars and cursed them out. It was one of my former friends, no less. I was so ruthless that I made the guy cry. Truth be told, this had nothing to do with money. Someone tried to step in on his behalf. In the heat of anger, I said, "Butt out! I could ruin your entire social life. Yeah, that's what I thought." I paused for a few seconds to ponder what I had just said. I couldn't believe that really came out of my mouth. I had never been a temperamental person; this was clearly getting out of hand. After being picked on for years, I had turned into the very thing I hated. I had officially become a bully.

My long-time friends got wind of the awful things I was doing. They were ticked off, and rightfully so. They decided it was time to confront me. They did so with respect and discretion. When I left practice, they were waiting at the top of the gym stairwell. They waited for the rest to leave, then calmly asked, "Why are you doing this? I don't see what your problem is. I really don't know what we did to you." I didn't know how to respond because I didn't have an answer. All they wanted me to do was apologize and change my ways. I had a chance to save those friendships. In my arrogant pride, I refused to do it. I wouldn't budge an inch. I was too self-absorbed to listen to logic or reasoning. I didn't even admit to being in the wrong. One of them nudged the others and mumbled, "I told you he would act like this!" They said that their folks did not want them around me if I acted this way. The parents had already agreed on this. It appeared that this conversation had been planned ahead of time. My lifelong friends tried to talk some sense into me before giving up. They complained that I was becoming a bad influence.

I rolled my eyes and said, "Do you know who you're talking to? Look around you. Listen to all those people in the stands who adore me! In case you haven't noticed, I am a freaking star around here. I'm getting more popular by the minute. Y'all are making a big mistake. Don't come crying to me when I'm the king of this school, and you're still sitting at the nerd table! I'm the one who's winning here. The whole school is on my side. I can do anything I want, and they will still love me!"

Andrew started to back away along with the group. He did the best he could to hold it together. He uttered, "I really hope you're right about that last part." He sighed and looked at the floor. His voice seemed genuinely concerned. A crowd walked by as he said this. I put my sunglasses on and smirked back. "Damn straight I am! You just watch and see. I don't need you anyway!" Despite my sassy comeback, the crowd hardly noticed. They didn't even slow down to look at me. They were busy chatting among themselves. That little show I put on was a whole lot of nothing. I lost my closest friends and got nothing out of it.

They waxed the basketball court overnight, and it looked super shiny the next day. I sprang off the bench and got into the zone. I was ready to give that crowd a show they would remember. The starter waved for me to join them as they practiced a play. I moved near the three-point line. The center guy got swamped, so he chucked the ball my way. The defense didn't try that hard to block me. I had an open shot. The point guard looked at me and smirked as he raised one brow. He pointed at the basket and said, "Go ahead, Joey! Nobody's stopping you! Let's see what you've got." The others got quiet and looked at me. The whole gym got quiet. My blood pressure rose. I could practically feel everyone staring at me. The starter backed away, assuming that I would crack under the pressure and miss the shot. He put his hand up in preparation to grab the rebound. I tuned everything out for a second and looked straight at the square on the backboard. I jumped up and gracefully flicked the ball. Not too hard and not too light. My Nike shoes slammed onto the court, and we all waited. They nonchalantly watched it fly over their heads. It was looking good, but I thought it would land short. I bit my lip with angst. The net flapped, and the crowd roared. The team raised their hands and ruffled the starter's tee shirt. They said, "Oh wait! He swished it! That didn't even touch the backboard! You sure underestimated him, didn't you?" I let the energy from the crowd go straight to my mouth. I yelled out, "Yeah, that's right! I'm the freaking shit! Don't even act like I'm not!" A cocky smirk came naturally. I mumbled, "Man, this is freaking great!"

Everyone was cheering and going crazy, except the people who knew me best. They knew better. My former friends were sitting halfway up the bleachers. I could see them out of the corner of my eye. They had their arms crossed as they watched me. Andrew raised his hands and looked down at me. I could read his lips. His eyes got narrow as he exclaimed, "Why, Joey?" The rest of them shook their heads in disappointment. I couldn't look at them. The shame was too strong. I looked down, but I could still see them in the reflection on the court.

The awkward tension threw me off. I was usually a good defense player, but the ball kept getting away from me. Everything seemed to be happening faster than normal. I kept zoning out and losing a step. My reactions were behind by a fraction of a second. I caught myself pacing around the court in a pattern. My ears got hot. My hands were frail and fidgety. I asked one of the guys on the bench to take over for me. I walked to the coach's office to chug down a bottle of Gatorade. When I couldn't see the crowd, the fidgeting stopped. I didn't get it. I walked back out and felt the tension come rushing back. My eyes went straight to my old friends' group. I didn't understand why I still cared what they thought; they weren't my friends at this point.

Someone told me that losing friends was a natural part of becoming popular. I was warned that some people would be jealous of my success. This kind of jealousy would lead to them not taking it very well. They told me, "Haters are going to hate." I convinced myself that is all this was. I figured it meant I had outgrown them. I assumed my best chances were to double down and keep going.

Later that day, somebody approached my locker. "Hey, Joey, I heard what happened. Those guys you used to hang out with are history. They might be content with mediocrity, but not you! You don't want anything to do with those guys. You made the right call." I shrugged back, "Yeah, they wanted me to become a watered-down version of myself. I wasn't having it! I have a life now, and I'm not giving that up just to please three or four people. Where's the logic in that? They weighed me down for years. Now it's MY time!" The other guy nodded his head with excitement. "There you go! Now you're talking!" He put his hand out for a fist bump. I played along. "Yeah, man, I should have done this years ago!" My mouth said one thing, while my heart was saying the opposite. I didn't really agree with what I was saying.

After lunch, we took our seats in the gym for a pep rally. I sat near the top with the rest of the basketball team. My former friends approached and tried to get me to come to my senses. They did so against their better judgment, at the dismay of their parents. People went after them like vultures for their efforts. They called them a bunch of names and threw their trash at them. I was so scared of what people would think of me if I intervened. I acted like I didn't even know them in order to please the crowd. From that day forward, I did not want to be seen anywhere near them. I knew they were starting to get picked on, but I never did anything. I feared that, if I stood up for them, I would be next. The ones that picked on them were the very people I wanted to get in good with. I wouldn't admit it, but it pained me to let that stuff go. All I could do was try to tune it out. Pretending I didn't know was the only way I could deal with it.

I failed them when they needed me the most. They finally learned that they were beating a dead horse. They quit trying to call me. That is when I learned that they were not bluffing. I went home and slung my bag into my room. I slouched into the kitchen and smelled pork chops. The table was already set. We sat down to eat like we always did. Suddenly, I was caught off-guard. Grandma said, "I haven't heard from Andrew and the rest of your friends for a while. Is everything okay between you guys?" I replied, "Well, actually, we had a difference of opinion." Her face was filled with disappointment. "That's really sad to hear. They've been your best friends for your whole life. If you throw that away, you are going to regret it." She was about to continue, but I cut her off. "Yeah, well, it's too late for that, okay? I already burned the bridge. There's no going back now." She shrugged and asked, "So who are you currently hanging with, then?" I chuckled and replied, "People who can get me what I want." She scrunched her nose and looked at me sternly. That wiped the smug smile off my face. I had an uneasy feeling inside. I knew better than to tell her more.

After practice, one of my new friends zig-zagged through the crowd to join me. He had a mischievous grin on his face. He whispered, "Dude, there is a sick ass party coming up that you have got to go to. You will get absolutely lit, my man!" I smirked and replied, "Keep talking. What does that mean?" He rolled his eyes and said, "Well, let me ask you a question first. Have you ever shot fireball?" I shook my head in confusion. He grabbed my sleeve and said, "Oh, we have got to have you try some shots! They'll probably have some cold ones and stuff too. It'll be a fun time." I froze in disbelief. "Wait, that means beer, right?" He flicked his hand and said, "Yeah, but most people will be doing the fun stuff. Are you feeling me?" He nudged me and laughed. I smiled and pretended that I knew what he was talking about. He pulled me aside to give the details. He said that the plan was to wait for his big brother to leave for vacation over the break. We would sneak into his room to grab the booze. Then we would go down to a friend's basement to throw the party. I was scared of what he would tell people if I turned down his offer. I didn't want to look like a scared wimp. I said, "Hell, yeah, brother, I'm in!"

I tasted one of Grandpa's beers in the garage out of curiosity. I wanted to know what I would be getting into if I went to the party. I opened it and got lightheaded when I smelled the foam. I took a slow sip and sloshed it around. I sprinted behind the garage to spit it out. I did not like the taste of it at all. I thought it might taste better the second time, so I took two big chugs. My throat and abs got tense like I was about to throw up. Afterward, my breath smelled gross. I couldn't stand it. I tried eating sweets to get the aftertaste out of my mouth. It took hours before it finally went away. I no longer wanted to go to that party, but I also didn't want to disappoint my new friends. On the last school day before break, I pretended I was sick so I wouldn't have to go. I held my breath for a few moments so my face would be red. I told the guy that I couldn't make it to the party because I didn't want to kill the mood for everybody else. I tried to act disappointed and bummed out. I claimed that I would be down for the next one to put it off. I did a fake cough as I left the room. He seemed to buy it; that was quite a relief.

After we returned from break, I was called down to the principal's office. There was no warning or heads up. I had no clue what it was about. There was a litany of things it could have been. I tried to retrace my steps, but I didn't even know where to start. My feet were tapping uncontrollably. Something beeped on the receptionist's desk. Another kid came walking out. I tried to read the principal's mood, but I couldn't tell. Nothing seemed out of the ordinary. Nobody else was in his office, so that was a good sign. My biggest fear was having my grandparents called. That didn't seem likely, which gave me a little bit of comfort. I took a seat as he fixed his tie. He pulled his chair up. "Listen, Joey...I'm just going to say it. Some complaints have been brought to my attention. When I first saw these write-up sheets, I didn't believe what I was seeing. I followed up with the teachers to double-check. I thought perhaps they had made a mistake. I told them, 'There's no way he would do this, that's not the Joey I know.' What they told me next was very concerning to me. They felt that they couldn't trust you. You've changed and become someone that they don't know anymore. I don't get it. What happened to you?"

My throat dried up as I panicked. "I never thought it would go this far! It started out so innocent. I'm just going with the flow that the popular kids are setting. I know this has gotten out of hand, but I don't know how to put the cat back in the bag. I had no clue this is what I was signing up for."

He picked up his clipboard. He glanced at the write-up sheets and spun a pen around. "For what it's worth, I'm glad that the student body has accepted you. I really am. It probably feels great. I'm telling you, it's a dangerous game you're playing out there. I have seen it all, and nothing surprises me anymore. I know how brutal these kids can be. Sometimes it only takes one mistake to get on their bad side. My advice to you is this: Don't get so high and mighty that you start making stupid mistakes. Things may not always be like they are now. You really need to keep it in check. If you go down this road, I won't have any choice but to throw the book at you. I have a job to do. The district guidelines call for three days of detention. You need to decide how far you are willing to go." I knew he had a point, but I wouldn't admit it. I walked out of the office and put my sunglasses back on. I slowly walked back to class to allow time to breathe and calm myself down. I was so relieved that I didn't get questioned about the party. That was a close one.

I never thought popularity would change me. I didn't think it would change my moral standards or compromise my integrity. Little did I know that that was the price I would pay. Sometimes I wished I had never gotten a taste of the spotlight. If I didn't know how good it felt, I wouldn't have gone this far. I said some things that I thought I'd never say. The guilt got so strong that I often struggled to get out of bed in the morning. I didn't like who I was becoming. I so desperately wanted my mental innocence back.

By the world's standards, I should have been ecstatic. I had the life that I had always wanted. My peers held me in high esteem. Everyone wanted a slice of my attention. This was my ultimate revenge fantasy come to life. I was a comeback story beyond my wildest dreams. I thought my new life would buy me freedom, but it didn't. As I fell deeper into this lifestyle, I felt trapped. I had to stay hard and ruthless all the time. I could not show any vulnerability to my new friends. I knew they were not trustworthy. I couldn't take a break from my act, even for a second. Behind my tough exterior, I was more fearful than ever. I was scared to death of backsliding to who I was before. I feared getting caught or, worse, being exposed for who I really was. I knew that I was only one mistake away from losing everything I had worked for. None of that fame was enough to free me from life's anxiety. I was in a different type of bondage than I was used to, but nonetheless, it was still bondage. That was not what I had signed up for. I had no clue what my next move would be.

CHAPTER TEN — The Fabrication Game

S eventh-grade year was a non-stop party. People told me that I was a badass, and I believed them. It was a year filled with basketball games, camera flashes, and plenty of controversy. Despite the cost, this was the happiest I had ever been. Time flew when I was having fun; eighth grade was quickly approaching. As the popular kids grew older, the prestige of basketball faded. Puberty set in, and they suddenly had new priorities. I walked into class one day, but nobody looked up. They were too busy with their cell phones. This was extremely unusual. Several of my classmates were huddled together at the front of the room, whispering among themselves. They were discussing who was dating whom and who was "talking" to whom. The girls got excited and giddy. They whispered in high-pitched voices. It was like a popularity contest to them. Bragging rights were everything. "Having game" had nothing to do with basketball anymore. Dating was the next big thing. They asked me if I was talking to anybody, but I managed to change the subject.

My locker had love notes in it, with phone numbers and hearts on them. I didn't really care that girls were interested in me. I tossed most of the notes in the trash and never told anybody I got them. I had zero interest in dating. It all seemed like a big hassle. One of the notes was from a name I didn't recognize. I opened it up to figure out who it was. It was written in fancy cursive with teal blue ink. It said, "You probably don't know who I am, but I've wanted to meet you. It's just really scary. My name is Charlotte." I scratched my head. One of the popular kids came around the corner along with his comrades. He raised his hands in the air with surprise. "Woah there, JP! What in the hell do we have here? Who is the chick sending this to one of our boys?" I smirked and rolled my eyes. "Man, I don't know! I'm having a hard time keeping track of all these girls." They all laughed and patted me on the back. They banged on the locker next to mine and said, "We've got a player in the house! These chicks better watch out!" I was having a blast.

As we were talking, I saw a girl come around the corner. She was not wearing brand-name clothes. Her shoes were not Nikes, and her glasses were not made by Gucci. She didn't walk with a cocky swagger. It was almost like she didn't know how pretty she was. She humbly smiled at me and blushed as she got closer. Some of the guys saw her and instantly began catcalling. They made obscene gestures and spouted sexual innuendos. They licked their lips like she was a juicy steak for sale at the state fair. I was so disgusted that I couldn't look at those guys. I backed away out of fear. I didn't want to get pressured into joining them. She covered her face as she trotted past. While that was going on, another guy ruffled my shirt collar and exclaimed, "Dude, any chick that sends you a note like this is clearly lame! If she was hot, she wouldn't have to do this to get guys. You can do better than that. Come on now, don't you agree?" I caved in and said, "Duh, of course I agree! Who is Charlotte anyway?" They shredded the note and threw it in the trash. They patted me on the back again and said, "Who cares? She's obviously a loser, so it doesn't matter. I don't care what anybody says, you are the freaking man! Keep being you, JP." I didn't know where that last part had come from. After they all left, I went on my way. The girl looked back at me and seemed sad about something.

I passed by her on my way to my next class. She was curled up in a chair. She was covering her face with her hands. I couldn't tell if she was crying or not. I didn't want to risk looking stupid over nothing, so I kept walking down the hall.

I set my binders down on a desk and went to the bathroom to change. When I did, I eavesdropped on a conversation I wasn't supposed to hear. Two guys walked in. "...Dude, I've got like six or seven chicks' numbers in my phone right now. I'm going out with one tonight and another one tomorrow!" The other guy said, "Did you know that Joey doesn't have a girl yet?" "No way! The basketball player? That can't be true. Chicks love jerks like him, don't they?" "I don't know, man. I heard that he's actually insecure. It is all an act! He is not that confident in real life. Have you seen how he acts around the chicks?" They both lowered their voices. "Oh dude, he's totally faking it. He doesn't even know how to talk to girls! We'll get dates long before he does. How much do you want to bet that he's a virgin?" They exploded with laughter. They were hee-hawing so hard that they slapped the walls and almost cried. One of them sarcastically yelled, "Dude, shut up! I'm going to piss myself over here!" They couldn't control themselves.

Those guys thought they were alone in that bathroom, but they weren't. They had no clue I was in the stall. I stayed put until they left. I was no stranger to controversy, but never to this extent. This one felt like a shot across the bow. It hurt more than I care to admit. I felt a slice of my worth get ripped out of me. I thought about getting revenge, but I didn't want to blow my cover.

I had no desire to date before hearing that conversation. Now I desperately needed to. I had to prove them all wrong. I had to show them that I could do anything another man could do! That is what dating was all about for me. It was really just a quest to prove that I had the ability. This pushed me to start dating much sooner than I was comfortable with. I was hoping to put it off until late high school, but that wasn't going to fly. Like basketball, this was a new trend that I needed to capitalize on. I needed to get into the dating world early to stand a chance. It was the only way I'd be able to keep my status.

All of a sudden, I was comparing myself to other guys in the school. I saw them as my competition. I wore shirts that were way too tight, but I couldn't bring myself to toss them. I taught myself how to flex my arms and abs all the time. I didn't do this to the point where it was obvious, but just enough to feel good about myself. I ate smaller food portions to look skinnier. I constantly looked over my shoulder to see if my efforts were paying off. I put in all of that work just to prove a point.

I began brainstorming ideas. How could I make the biggest impact possible? I wanted to do something daring that no one else would even think about trying. I got it! If I dated a cheerleader, imagine how big that story would be. I thought, "That'll show them!" I chose my first crush strategically. This girl was one of the most popular cheerleaders in the school. Her friends had quite a following as well. They all had big personalities. They used the phrase, "Oh my God," quite often. This phrase could mean very different things, depending on how they said it. Their tone and eye rolls did most of the talking. They were not shy about telling it like it was. They did everything in a pack.

As a cocky guy, approaching this girl should have been a piece of cake. The truth is that it was not easy for me. I was terrified. I still had some autism-related weaknesses. This was a daunting hurdle to overcome. I needed to research and prepare myself. I was not about to take dating advice from my grandparents; that would be gross. I couldn't ask my teammates; they would think less of me! With no viable options, I turned to the internet. I signed up to be trained by a "licensed" pickup artist. That training course had absolutely awful advice. Catcalling was too gutsy for me. I can't even type these pickup lines with a straight face! The least awful one was, "Hey baby, your eyes are the same color as my daddy's Porsche!" I gagged at the thought of putting myself out there like that. I will not repeat the other pickup lines, because they were quite vulgar. If I couldn't even hold eye contact with the opposite sex, how would I say something like that? Eye contact felt incredibly uncomfortable. It was intimidating. I struggled to hold it for more than five seconds. It was my Achilles' heel.

In my infinite wisdom, I had an idea. I thought of a way to approach her with little eye contact at all. I got a folder and acted as if getting a date was like getting hired. I put in a makeshift resume with my basketball headshot, two poems, and a necklace from Walmart. What else signals to a girl that a guy has money like a plastic necklace with traces of Axe body spray? I also bought the latest Justin Bieber album in case I needed backup. This gave me a chance to mention that "I knew Justin's agent and had them set one aside for her." Real classy stuff, I know. I took a deep breath and moseyed over to her side of the hallway. I tried to explain my dilemma and get her friends rooting for me. They shrugged their shoulders as if to say, "Sorry, kid, you're on your own. Good luck!" She came around the corner. It was show time, and there was no turning back. I got more nervous than a cat in a room full of rocking chairs. I was so scared of messing up that, when I opened my mouth, no sound came out. I think they felt bad for me, which is why they didn't give me the boot. Her friends got weirded out and left us there. She neatly folded her cheer uniform and stowed it away. A strong perfume smell wafted outward as she opened her locker. I finally got the courage to start talking. Despite the unorthodox way that the conversation started, the look of surprise on her face eventually turned into a smile. Her eyes were on the folder by my design. I didn't have to hold eye contact, which made the silence bearable as I thought of what to say next. I spouted the presentation that I had practiced. I got a laugh, which meant I was doing better than I expected. It was still an awkward interaction, but it wasn't humiliating. To me, that was a success. I felt like my IQ was ridiculously high for thinking of this idea. I thought I was the most sophisticated man on Earth. I couldn't wait to tell my critics that I had proved them wrong.

I came to basketball practice with an extra pep in my step. "Hey, guess what I did yesterday?" My teammates were tying their Jordans and listening to iPods. "What's up, player?" "I put the moves on a cheerleader, and you've got to hear how I did it, y'all. I am a freaking genius!" They smiled at each other and took off the headphones. The point guard raised his chin and asked me who it was. He got bug-eyed when I told him. "Hold up, are you for real? You put the moves on her? Now I've got to hear this! How'd you do it?" Everyone huddled around for the details. I was pumped to see them making a fuss about me again. I enjoyed the moment so much that I didn't consider the aftermath.

Everyone was waiting for a juicy tale, so I gave them one! In the locker room version of the story, she was the one who got star-struck and speechless, not the other way around. I acted like I was James Bond, and she was swooning over me the instant I started talking. I told them I had used "advanced psychology" to manipulate her into approaching me first. I said it was all her idea, and she initiated the tango. The only problem with this was that it was not true. The longer I talked, the more they wanted to know. One guy put his hand up and said, "Heck yeah, boy, Joey over here has got game! Up top, big man!" I began improvising even further to keep their interest. That's a nice way to say that I was lying. I told a very different tale than the one that really took place. I got pats on the back and all kinds of praise. I blurted all this out during a moment of excitement. Some of my comrades pointed her out in the stands. They whispered in my ear, "Is that her?" Right then, the blinding euphoria went away. I got nervous and changed the subject. I was dumb enough to believe this story wouldn't spread. I never directly asked them to keep it a secret, but I anticipated that they would. I thought the locker room was a safe space where I could lie with zero consequences. Clearly, I was wrong.

I didn't know it yet, but the rumor was picking up steam all morning. The guys texted their friends, and they started texting theirs. It had a snowball effect. I would never in a million years have seen this coming. By the time it traveled back to the cheerleading team, it was a big disaster. I was messing with the wrong person. I strutted to class, oblivious to what was going on. I was planning to ask the cheerleader to the winter dance. As I entered the classroom, there was a group looking over her shoulder. They all stood up and confronted me at once. I tried to act stunned by their news as if I was hearing it for the first time. One of them yelled from the back, "Cut the crap, Joey! We know everything!" They were outraged. I looked down at the floor tiles and nervously crossed my arms. I mumbled under my breath, "Wait a second, how do they know?" Needless to say, they had some words for me after that. I think they were well deserved. They could tell that I was never interested in her for noble reasons. They exposed my true colors. I was surrounded and vastly outnumbered. There was no way to escape this or play it off. It looked bad because it was. They could have said and done so much more than they did. I was conceited and bound to lock horns with someone eventually; It was only a matter of time. In hindsight, I needed to be humbled before I did something even more stupid. Who knows what I would've tried next if I got away with this? I'll never know. For the first time in a year, my mouth stopped running.

The incident forced me to confront my extreme pride. This mistake was so much bigger than just me. I wasn't the heartless villain I wanted everyone to believe I was. The truth was that I still cared. I genuinely felt bad for the fallout I had caused the cheerleader. I wanted to make things right. I decided to go apologize. I was hoping to do so when our nosy peers weren't around, but I didn't get that chance. I only had mere seconds as I walked past the car line. I said my piece and hoped I was doing the right thing. She put it behind her as though it had never happened. She handled it with much more class than I had up to that point. Unfortunately, our peers were not as mature as her. Once they saw me talking to her, those middle school kids were ruthless. A mob of them watched me leave. I couldn't get one second of peace. Every class, every hallway, every hour, and every minute was consumed with talk about the incident. I was not prepared to cope with the aftermath. I didn't think there would be an aftermath! It was getting really bad. I didn't know what to do.

I hung out for a while in the locker room the next morning. When it got quiet, I thought it was safe to go out. I tied my shoes and put my headphones on. I turned my music up loud to drown out the embarrassment. I grabbed a basketball and dribbled my way down the corridor. I couldn't hear anything over the AC/DC blasting in my ears. I charged around the corner, thinking the stands were empty. I quickly realized that the crowd was still there. The team was standing in a row on the sideline. People were setting up a microphone in the center of the court. The principal was coming to speak in a few minutes. I took one of my headphones out and noticed that the gym was completely silent. Everyone heard me dribbling and running out. Several girls in the stands pointed at me and whispered among themselves. My foot hit a divider on the floor. I nearly tripped and fell. I had to leap forward and catch myself. This caused my shoes to slam on the court. It was very loud. My headphones ripped out of my ears and slid across the court. Everyone was staring at me. One of my teammates scrunched his nose with anger. He grunted out, "Dude, seriously, stop!" I set the ball down on the court and put my hands up. "Okay, okay...sorry!" I crouched down and waddled forward to pick up my headphones. Someone yelled from the stands, "Get out of here!" I stood and slowly backed up. As I did, the crowd started clapping and cheering. Many were laughing at me; some booed. They rejoiced as I walked away.

I sat back down in the locker room and stayed there. I didn't bother going back to get my headphones. I never wanted to go out onto that court again. I lost my motivation to play. It wasn't the same anymore. A teammate came in and slapped the doorframe. I stood up to stretch. He said, "The principal's done. Why aren't you out there doing the drills?" I sighed and mumbled, "Honestly, I have a lot of personal stuff to deal with. I can't look at all those people in the stands right now." He snapped his fingers to demand my attention. He pointed at me. "You, sir, just lost my respect! If you're not going to get out there and earn your spot, you might as well leave. You're taking up a space on this team that should go to someone who cares. There's nothing left for you here." I stared at a crack in the concrete. A mix of guilt, fear, and hopelessness all hit at once. I lay on the bench and hoped things would be better with the rest of the team. An hour or so later, they came in and switched to their outdoor shoes. I sat up and asked how practice went, but I got no answer. Nobody looked at me or said a word to acknowledge my existence. They acted completely indifferent toward me. I felt invisible. The coaches didn't look at me the same way anymore, either. That is when I knew it was all over. I had no reason to stay. I moseyed to the office and requested a schedule change.

Before I knew it, I was watching from the bleachers once again. I sat down and saw a bunch of stunned faces looking at me. Some people had their hands over their mouths to hide their giggling. "What are you doing here?" I took a deep breath and said it out loud for the first time. "I quit the team." That moment was painful. It felt like a demotion. I had been royalty, but I had lost the palace. It took me a whole year to gain that popularity, but only one week to lose it.

I tried to make conversation with someone in the stands. "That guy in the red hoodie was always my favorite teammate. He's good at defense." The guy to my right exasperated and rolled his eyes. "Why are your lips moving, dude? Nobody's listening to you. Just shut up for once!" Several people laughed and nodded in agreement. I said, "I wasn't talking to you! What's your problem, anyway?" He raised his hands. "Remember when you called me a wimp and made everyone laugh at me?" I sighed and looked down at my shoes. "...Yeah, I remember that, but I'm surprised you do. I said what the crowd wanted me to say." He put his headphones on and mumbled, "Could've fooled me! You only care about yourself and your image. Just stay away!" He scooted down from me. Everybody around us scooted away also. The row below me moved down. Everyone above me climbed up. I had a small section of the bleachers to myself. I stretched out my legs and made myself comfortable. I put my hands to my head and lay down. Everyone shook their heads in disgust. "What?" Several people yelled in unison, "Shut up!"

I walked to class and avoided eye contact. I sat in the back and stayed silent. The popular kids walked in and whispered among themselves. One of them stood up and shouted, "Joey, why are you still wearing your basketball hoodie? You might as well quit living in the past and accept reality! You are not worthy to represent the basketball team anymore." My voice cracked as I replied. "Yeah, well, I never asked you!" Everyone laughed and mimicked my voice. I took off my team gear, lost the sunglasses, and threw my hands up. "Are you happy now?" He put his hand to his chin. "Almost, but you're still here!" I had no retort to that. I sat down and gave it a rest.

I kept a low profile and waited it out. I expected the shame to fade with time. Several weeks went by, but the feeling of exile only grew stronger. The loss of basketball left a massive void. I felt a deep sense of withdrawal. It stung so bad to know how good life could be yet watching it slip away. It wouldn't have hurt so bad if I didn't know what I was missing. Unfortunately, I knew it all too well. It was impossible to forget. I was in a school filled with people but more alone than ever before. I was banished from all social circles. Most people stayed away from me to avoid being mistaken as my friend.

I was getting desperate for someone to talk to, anybody at all. I wanted someone to come along and save me from my shame and loneliness. Perhaps finding a girlfriend would be the answer to all of my problems. The couples at school appeared to be happy with their lives, so it was only logical. I got busy asking out several girls per week. I got shot down every time. I lost more of my social momentum. I started wondering if I would ever come back from this.

The student council taped neon flyers everywhere. The winter dance was coming in a few weeks. This event was an absolute must. If my peers saw me with a date, maybe they would start talking to me again. Perhaps that would tip the scales in my favor. I asked a girl from my church that I didn't know very well. Miraculously, I got a yes. I was ecstatic. Finally, someone had agreed to go with me! This was my last hope. I couldn't wait for the dance to arrive. I was so ready to start my life over.

After the tenth breath mint and a ridiculous amount of Axe body spray, it was show time. I was so nervous about what people were going to think. It was freezing cold outside. My nose was burning. We could see our breath. I could only imagine how those girls in paper-thin skirts were feeling. Everyone crowded the door. My face got as pale as the sidewalk. We went in, and several people noticed my date. They looked pretty shocked. They could hardly believe it. I went to the restroom and heard someone say, "I have no idea what that girl sees in you. Cheers! You are going to screw this up, so you better enjoy it while it lasts." I went back to the table and nervously looked around. I tried to act confident, but it was hard to do. Some of my old friends came by and chatted for a few minutes. That was progress in the right direction, but not much. The popular kids still seemed a hundred miles away. I tried chatting with my old basketball pals, but they turned away. They acted as if they never knew me.

My date got up with her friends and walked out to the dance floor. She motioned for me to follow. I couldn't make myself get up. I was too nervous. My heart was thumping. A few minutes later, she came back out of the auditorium. "What are you doing back here? All of the fun is over there! You came here to dance, right?" I nervously shook my head. "I have no clue what I'm doing. I can't afford to embarrass myself! Not again. I'm already walking on thin ice with these people." Her eyebrows lowered. "What are you talking about?" I finished my drink and shrugged it off. I mumbled under my breath. "You know what? Never mind. Maybe it's best that you don't know that."

I forced myself to get up and act confident. I was actually terrified the whole night. Luckily though, the neon lights hid it pretty well. Every few seconds, I looked around to see if anyone had noticed me. I circled around the room and showed her off to start conversations. I didn't really want to be there. However, the show had to go on. I thought it was my last chance to save my reputation.

I got exhausted. My social battery was drained. I sat down for the last part of the night. One of her friends pulled up a chair. "What's up with you? Something is clearly going on, so spill." I took in a deep breath. "This is not going how I thought it would." She raised her eyebrows and sighed with disappointment. "Why not? What's wrong with her? She looks beautiful in that dress!

Are your eyes working?" I looked down at the floor. "It's not her. It's my whole life. This is not how I expected my life to go. I don't understand any of it. I'm stumped." She smirked and put her hand up. "Amen, preach it, bro. I hear that!" I high-fived her and smiled to relieve the awkwardness. The truth is, I wasn't kidding around. Nobody knew what was going on inside my head.

My date and I hung out and called each other boyfriend and girlfriend for a few months. The whole time, I reeked of desperation. She started getting clues that I was not as confident as I originally let on. We didn't stay together very long. My insecurities led to petty arguments, which then led to bigger arguments. She ended the relationship in the most mature way possible. Nonetheless, I still got ticked off and resentful. I thought she had taken away my chances of having a social life. Truth be told, she had dodged a bullet. A bullet that was picking up speed. I just didn't know it yet.

Chapter Eleven — The Reason

My hope of returning to a high status was not looking good. It became clear that I would not be popular again for a long time, if ever. Crowds of people used to approach me. Now I had no meaningful friendships, and my ex-girlfriend had already moved on. My safety net was no longer in place. I was a prime target after leaving the basketball life. I had gotten so accustomed to popular treatment that I had grown complacent. I no longer knew how to hold my own in those hallways. This made me a sitting duck. I could feel my vulnerability catching up to me. I finally learned what bullying was all about.

A guy snuck up behind me and grabbed my bag strap. He slung me into the lockers. My books and drawings fell everywhere. He stepped on them with muddy boots as he raced off. "Dude, you're always in the way! Nobody even wants you here!" People around us giggled with haughty derision. They didn't show a single ounce of remorse. They watched it happen and did nothing.

A teacher came around the corner shortly after. She offered to help me pick up my things. I hesitantly nodded. One of the bystanders fixed her ponytail and whispered in my ear, "Nobody believes a word you say anymore, so...yeah. Snitching won't change a thing. Don't even bother trying." She smiled from ear to ear. I exclaimed to the teacher, "Did you hear that?" "...Hear what?" "Never mind, I guess." People flipped me off as they left. I got more furious and exclaimed, "Let me guess, you didn't see that either, did you?" The teacher finally looked up, handed me my binders, and said, "What are you talking about?" I shrugged my shoulders and gave it a rest.

The war had officially returned, stronger than ever. I had to watch my back. People were shooting spitballs, throwing trash wads, and everything in between. They randomly punched and shoved me around for no reason. I almost got into several fights, but luckily, they never happened. I managed to stall them and get saved by the bell. The bullies got to plan their moves. They conveniently timed it right when there were no teachers or cameras around. I, on the other hand, did not have that luxury. I simply reacted. Teachers and peers only saw half of what was really going on. I knew how it would look if I fought back. If I retaliated, I would be the bad guy. I endured it and didn't try to seek help. I wasn't getting into fist fights, so I thought I was handling it. Each day was a little rougher than the last.

There was an alley between two school buildings. It was the shortest way to my fourth-hour class. I walked through and heard a chain clinking behind me. Naturally, I turned around to find the source. Two guys got a grip and sent me flying into the concrete wall. One of them smiled and said, "How about you stay home this time and never come back?" I froze. I used to believe I was a big and tough guy, but not right now. I had no clue what to say for several seconds. I got so scared that my bottom jaw tingled. My legs felt like Jell-O. I had to catch my breath. There was no one in sight who could help me. I finally shook my head and replied, "Do you remember what you said to me the day after I joined basketball? You said that you were on my side! You actually had some decency back then. I almost started respecting you! What happened to that?" He rolled his eyes and said, "Well, I'm not as good of a liar as you!" Everyone smiled and booed me as he said this. He kept going. "I'm clearly not as stupid as you, either! Did you really think people ever liked you? They never did! They only put up with you because of your basketball pals. Those days are over, junior! You are nothing. Do you hear me? NOTHING! Don't you ever forget that!" He shoved me back into the wall. Braxton smiled with delight as he walked by. He motioned for the group to follow him. I closed my eyes and took a deep breath. The guy whispered in my ear before taking off, "They were using you the whole time. Now, this school is done with you." When I opened my eyes, they were gone. I waited for the rest of the bystanders to leave.

I told a teacher some of what was happening, but not all of it. I left out most of the details. I didn't want to poke the bear and look like a snitch. I asked what she would do in my position. She paused and looked at the floor. "There is no easy way to say this, but you have a bit of a reputation. Word on the street is that you've been telling some nasty lies. If you want people to like you again, you need to show some integrity. It's their word against yours, and, quite frankly, your word is not that good right now. That can change, but you've got some work to do." It took every bit of my strength not to break down. I knew it was my fault no one trusted me. I made my bed, so now I had to lie in it. I accepted my fate and never asked for help again; I knew I was on my own.

I told everybody I was fine to get them off my back. It became less true each time I said it. I was far from fine. It had been almost a year since the cheerleader incident. Despite this, my peers treated me as if it had just happened. I couldn't live it down. The struggle began following me home. I stayed up late every night, planning my conversations with bullies. I turned the stereo up loud, so nobody heard me rehearsing. I had constant nightmares in which I had to fight for my life. Just as I escaped, I woke up gasping for air. I could hardly breathe for several seconds. My chest was tight, and my face nearly turned blue. It was a helpless feeling. All I could do was wait for the anxiety to pass. It felt so real that I couldn't tell the difference between nightmares and real life. I had a type of exhaustion that couldn't be slept off; if only it were that easy.

A tightness was developing in my forehead. My mind was lagging like a crappy internet connection. It took me longer to do basic tasks. Even thinking became too much work. I felt like crap. I just wanted to be left alone. I got on the bus before sunrise, hoping to sleep a little, but it wasn't possible. The gravel roads shook the bus too violently. An older girl climbed aboard and sat in front of me. Her kid brother followed. I lay as far down in the seat as I could. He threw trash wads my way for several minutes. They made a pile in the corner of my seat. He was making a high-pitched moaning voice. It was so loud that it made my ears hurt. It was making my headache worse by the second. He repeatedly yelled, "That's what your mom said last night!" He stuck his tongue out at everyone and grabbed a speaker from his bag. He plugged it into his new iPhone and turned his rap music as loud as it would go. His sister put her headphones on and ignored it. I grabbed the pile of paper wads and set them down on his seat. I calmly said, "Can you please turn that down a bit? It's giving me a headache." He gave a big smile and spat in my face. He crossed his arms and yelled, "Make me, dipstick! Nobody asked you!" I raised my hand and pointed him out to the bus driver as I wiped the saliva off my cheek. The driver yelled, "You turn that off right now and pick up your trash! You're sitting up front." He threw one of the wads at the driver and yelled, "Make me, woman! You ain't going to do shit!" She slammed the brakes and stopped the bus, refusing to go again until he adhered to her command. Everyone looked at him with contempt. He rolled his eyes and confidently strutted to the front. He apologized to his friends for making them wait, but not to anybody else.

His sister got a stern expression and said, "Really? You had to snitch on my little brother? You are absolutely worthless! If he gets written up, they will kick him off the bus. We can't afford to drive him. If he gets kicked off, so help me; I'll make your life a living hell!" She turned around and saw the bags under my eyes. She suddenly beamed with excitement. "Hey, everybody, look at this! He has dark circles under his eyes like a raccoon does! No wonder he's such a pest. It probably has rabies or something. Hopefully, it goes and dies in a hole somewhere." Everyone laughed...hard. I didn't want to think negative thoughts, but they were getting very powerful. Something came into my mind that threw me off. "If I weren't here, none of this would be happening. I wouldn't have to put up with it anymore." This caught me off-guard. Thoughts like this had never crossed my mind before. I figured it was just a one-time thing, so I brushed it off. It could have been a false alarm. Everyone has a brain fart occasionally. I shook my head to snap myself out of it.

The next day, this idea returned. It was much more detailed this time. I imagined that I was invisible, but I could see everyone else. I strolled through the hallways and heard every conversation. The bullies were looking all over the place, but they couldn't find me. They opened my locker only to see that it was empty. They moved on and found somebody else to pick on. The school hardly noticed that I was gone. The bullying had finally come to an end. It was all over. This seemed pretty nice.

Someone slammed their books down on the desk behind me. It made me flinch. My imagination stopped, and I snapped back to reality. I turned around and looked behind me. A guy with long hair made a static noise like a walkie-talkie radio. "Earth to Joey... you're still a dumbass, over!" A few people chuckled at that. He raised his arms and clenched his fists. "What are you going to do about it? Do you want to go? Do you want to fight, big Joe? My face is right here, you big wuss! You're not even going to try?" I didn't have the energy to argue anymore. I just let it be. I buried my face in my jacket. The bully laughed and exclaimed, "Jeez! It's like this dude is dead or something!" I mumbled under my breath, "Yeah, if only."

The teacher turned the corner and walked in for class. "What's so funny?" "Oh, nothing that concerns you, princess!" The teacher smirked and replied, "You're in a good mood! Why is that?" "Oh, I just love it when people are put in their place. Some people are idiots nowadays, don't you think?" "Amen to that, sister!" "...Hey Joey, wake up. Sleep on your own time." The bully yanked my jacket out from under me and made my head hit the desk. He put the jacket on top of me and sat back down. The teacher smiled and lightheartedly said, "Hey now, watch it! Let's get class started here. Take your binders out." I thought to myself, "What am I even doing here? I don't know why I try anymore. This is hopeless!" I wouldn't admit it, but my mental health was rapidly declining. My experiences with bullies were starting to mess with my psyche.

I sat near the back of the bus on the ride home. Braxton came to the back, too. "Get the hell up, fool." "...I was here first. All the seats behind me are empty." He crossed his arms and asserted, "I believe we have a misunderstanding. I wasn't asking!" He threw me into the adjacent seat. I got mad and punched his arm. I hit it with all of my might, but he didn't bat an eye. It was like he barely even felt it. My fist was hurting, but he seemed just fine. His arms were nearly a foot in diameter. He turned around and pump-faked a punch. I jumped back so hard that my head slammed into the window. I braced my arm and head as he laughed. There were people standing in the aisle because the bus was getting so full. The driver couldn't see either of us. When the bus started rolling, Braxton said, "You are not getting away with this. I'm going to hit you back. Do you want it to be now or at a random time of my choosing? You've got until the highway to decide. You better think fast, skippy." He crossed his arms and smiled the whole time. At the next stop, most people disembarked. I moved one seat back while I had the chance. He followed. "Time's up, junior. I'll go easy on you if you do it now. What's it going to be?" He slowly inched my way. I panicked and said, "All right, fine! Fair is fair. Will you leave me alone afterward?" He nodded his head.

I turned to put my binders away in my bag. Before I could, I saw a dark shadow coming at me. My head couldn't keep up with my body. A wave of heat shot up my arm. The pain hit about two seconds later. It felt like a million red wasps were stinging me at once. I had to hold my arm; my body did not give me a choice. There was a small dent in the metal where my shoulder had hit. "We're even, punk!" "...What the hell! You said you would go easy!" He smiled and said, "I did! If that's all it takes to get you down, you are not going to make it. You might as well kill yourself before someone does it for you."

I rolled my eyes and sarcastically said, "Ha-ha, nice try. You don't get to decide that." He got serious and replied, "I wasn't kidding. You'd be doing yourself a favor. Not everybody is going to make it in this world. Some people are just not good enough." He patted me on the head like a dog and strutted up the aisle. His chain necklaces were clinking as he left. Another bus pulled up while we were stopped at the elementary school. The little kids were excited to see him. They opened their windows and waved for Braxton to come. He spat on the ground and fixed his hair. Nobody else saw the side of him that his other victims and I did. He was smart enough to be careful when and how he unleashed it. I considered snitching on him to expose the charade once and for all. There was one problem with that plan. I already had two disciplinary strikes on my office record. If the principal found out that I threw the first punch, it would not have been good for me. I got out my student handbook and studied the fine print. From what I read, it seemed there was a 50/50 chance that I'd be suspended if I came forward. Those were not good odds to me. Grandma would have torn my butt to shreds if I got suspended. I wasn't even curious what Grandpa would do. I didn't care to find out. I was much more scared of suspension than I was of Braxton, so I decided to let the incident go.

I figured that I just needed to wait a little longer, then this would all blow over. I didn't tell people what was happening because of denial. I refused to face the urgency of the situation. As time went on, I gradually lost my desire to eat. People stole things off my lunch tray when I wasn't looking. It got to a point where I hardly ate at all. The feeling of starving was oddly comforting. If I could feel the pain, I knew I had made it another day. This gave me temporary wins over my mind's desire. Thoughts of suicide were building but at a very slow rate. They were manageable, so I did not take them seriously. I figured if they ever got out of hand, I would see it coming. I kept kicking the can down the road and waiting for the storm to end. I didn't want to believe that my mental health was in peril.

One night, I had a very detailed dream. I was being escorted through a concrete hallway. The floor was dirty with ash, and there were cracks in the ceiling. Smoke was oozing out of them. I had shackles on my hands and feet. A huge stone door opened to reveal a cliff on the other side. I could feel immense heat coming from the cliff. A yellow glow shimmered on the rock face. People were screaming, but they were very far away. I could barely hear them over the metal clanking. The prison guards took the shackles off and left. The stone door closed behind me. The sky was pitch-black. I walked to the edge of the cliff and looked down. The drop was several miles. At the bottom, there was fire. The screams sounded so bad that my jaw clenched. It was the most awful sound I had ever heard. My eyes stung from the heat, and my nose was burning from the ash smell. All of my senses were overloaded. I covered my ears and uttered, "This must be hell!" Suddenly, my stomach dropped. I felt like I was falling.

I kicked myself awake and gripped the bed with all of my strength. My palms became numb. I sat up once I finally caught my breath. I covered my ears to drown out the screaming, but there was no relief. No matter how loud I turned up the TV or my music, I could still hear it. Nothing worked. Every curse word and insult I ever said was playing over and over. The bullies' words were playing, too. My brain was screaming at me in every way imaginable. It persisted all night and day. I felt like I was trapped in a brain and body that were not my own. I often asked myself if this battle was worth fighting. The more I thought about ending things, the more tempting it became. I seriously considered it on day two. When I got home, I was too scared to follow through. I shook it off and convinced myself that this wasn't really happening. Nobody wanted to believe that I would do this; I also refused to believe it. I still had hope that things would improve if I just waited one more day. I thought I was still in control, but I was fooling myself.

The emptiness inside of me was so deep that I became emotionally numb. I didn't care about the things that previously gave me joy. Nothing felt good anymore. My whole existence was reduced to empty routines. An entire week passed, and the internal screaming still hadn't let up. The lack of sleep caused physical pain. My neck and back were throbbing. My limbs ached all over. A droning pain in my forehead would not stop. My eyes were stinging dry. There were instances where I nearly had a seizure from the sleep deprivation. I hadn't eaten a full meal in days, and it showed. I used to bench-press heavy weights, but now I struggled to lift my own backpack on certain occasions. The intensity of the pain and bullying ramped up with each day; I could no longer fight back. They became more than I could handle. I needed relief, even if it cost me my life. The despair had to end. I cleaned out my locker to save the custodians a little trouble. I left my textbooks in the classroom and emptied my binders. I don't think I said a single word that day. Our class was released early. Everybody raced out of the building to get a head start. They tripped over each other as they jockeyed for position. I was in no hurry. I strolled through the hall and looked at the dents in the lockers. I could see the spots where my jacket zipper had scratched the paint. I went through the alleyway and heard the bell ring. I left the school for what I thought was the last time.

It was a weeknight, which meant I was the first one home. All of the lights were off. The house was warm, but waves of cold came over me like the tide at a beach. My ears were thumping like drums. I shut the drapes in my grandparent's room and reached under the bed. I found what I was looking for and started pulling. A box tipped over, spilling out shotgun shells. The room was nearly pitch-black, so I couldn't see much. I finally touched the cold metal barrel.

My whole body trembled with fear. Every muscle ached from the shaking. I fought hard, but I was still gasping for air. The breaths felt empty. I was too dizzy to stand up. Everything got blurry, and I ended up on the floor. The panic was closing in on me. It was worse than it had ever been. I didn't want to do this, but my brain was convinced that it had to. My fingers had minds of their own. Every fiber in my being wanted to pull the trigger and get this over with. The desire was taking control; I was about to give in. As a final act of desperation, I cried out with everything I had, "God, I'm sorry! Please forgive me! If you save me, I'll do anything you want!" Begging was the only choice I had left. By now, I was choking on my own breath. I lost all willpower to resist the urge. I bowed my head and accepted that this was the end.

There was a bold thump in my chest. It was a very hard jolt, as if someone smacked me with all of their might. The force of it radiated through my body like a shockwave. As the sensation hit, my eyes bolted open. The surprise forced me to pause. That is when I felt a voice start to speak.

"Don't you DARE do this! I have a reason!"

Each word was spoken with extremely high authority. The power behind them was felt by my entire body. It was a force that was bigger than any human being. It resembled nothing on Earth, which makes it very hard to describe or explain. The voice wasn't physically audible; it was much more personal than that. Something led me to respect its authoritative nature. After those words were said, my natural response was to follow orders. I looked down and saw that the gun hadn't gone off. I realized that I was still alive, and it wasn't too late. I quit pressing on the trigger and eased my fingers off it.

Sunlight hit the drapes and lit the room. I felt a comforting warmth inside. Every hair on my head stood tall. I got goosebumps. The panic was cast out, and my brain stopped screaming. I was no longer gasping for air. Best of all, my pain was taken away. That amazing relief was too much to contain. I couldn't hold back the tears. The harder I tried, the stronger they became. I just couldn't stop. The smile on my face was not voluntary. I didn't see a supernatural being, but I saw enough. I could feel God's loving presence in that room. A sentiment that kept echoing was, "This is not the end!" Every aspect of the experience reaffirmed this message.

I did not know what to do with all of the glee and happiness I got from God's presence; it was an overdose of both. I went from having unbearable pain to no pain at all. This was the most joyful moment of my life. I had never experienced something like that before. When the sobbing quit, I started regaining my strength. I had a sudden strong desire to get up. I felt more alive than I had in years. My brain did not operate the same way it had in the past. I started perceiving life differently. Things would never be the same. I became a believer. I knew that there was definitely a Higher Power.

Grandma was supposed to be in a meeting for another hour, but the garage door was opening. She was feeling uneasy, so she rushed home. I couldn't cover my tracks in time. The shells rolled around as she stumbled to find the light switch. She was at a loss for words. She paced around with her hands over her mouth. She shook her head like she didn't want to believe what she was seeing. She gathered her composure and held her hand out. I handed her the gun. She unloaded it and rolled a bedsheet over it. She remained strong until we made eye contact, then came the waterworks. She sat on the bed and spoke up. "I knew something wasn't right, but I didn't want to smother you. I knew you wouldn't want that. Thank God I got here when I did!" I wanted to comfort her and stop the tears, but I didn't know how to. I wished she hadn't seen anything. We both got up and tried to put it behind us.

The sun was almost down, so I went to clean the mess off my bed. Grandma stormed to my door. I turned the knob and lay down. She slowly came in and motioned for me to sit up. She got her phone out. "I just checked today's voicemail messages. There's one from your number. I'm going to push play, and I need you to help me make sense of this. I'm clearly out of the loop." She put it on speaker. My voice sounded shaky. "Grandma, just so you know, I love you. What I'm about to do is not your fault. It's that damned school. I tried so hard, but it was never good enough for them. You have no clue what I've been through. Honestly, my life ended a long time ago."

With tears in her eyes, she pressed her lips together. "Just last week, you claimed to be fine. How did it go this far?" I finally spewed my guts. "Let me ask you something. Have you ever been thrown into a locker before? Have you lived with the fear of getting randomly punched in the hall for no reason? When people walk by, do you check your bags and pockets to make sure everything is still there? Have people joked about you being dead and told you to kill yourself? What kind of life is that? You. Don't. Get it. Most people will never get it, and I'm glad they don't."

There was a dusty Bible sitting on my nightstand. I hadn't touched it in years. I looked at it and said, "For what it's worth, I changed my mind after I sent that message. I couldn't actually do it. I heard this voice telling me to stop." My bottom lip shook as I continued talking. "It was SO powerful. It is really hard to explain. I'm still trying to figure out what that was."

She smiled and said, "Why don't you tell me? I think you know exactly what that was. I'm just grateful that you decided to listen." She raised her hands and said, "Speaking of which, are you finally ready to go back to the psychologist?" "Wait, I have a choice?" She crossed her arms and snapped back. "Actually, no. I'm making an appointment, and you will go." I smiled back and mumbled, "There it is. That's the Grandma I know!"

Going back to Dr. Mac's office was not what I wanted, but it was very much needed. I kept going every Friday for several months. During that time, several bullies changed school districts, got suspended, or both. Braxton moved to a bigger city, so the worst one was gone. Those who remained probably toned it down to avoid the juvenile detention center. I wasn't their only target, so they could have been in trouble for several incidents. I'll never know for sure. In hindsight, I was so glad that I hung around long enough to see the light at the end of the tunnel. Brighter days lay ahead of me. Little did I know that miracles can happen.

Things were looking up, but there was still unfinished business. I only told 70% of the truth. I was concerned that people would think I was insane if I disclosed the other 30%. I didn't want to be institutionalized for something I wasn't going through anymore. It didn't make sense to re-open a wound that had already started healing. I was careful to word things in a way that sounded as if I never lost control. I kept the truth under wraps for a long time. I went on and left it behind. Out of sight, out of mind. I intended to keep it a secret for the rest of my life.

CHAPTER TWELVE — Sorry, Starting Over

I t was time to change my lifestyle choices, but I didn't know where to start. I had a lot of questions. I got up early on the weekend and walked to the porch. A trail of cigarette smoke led to the table. I needed to talk to the one man who had my ear. I pulled up a chair and said that my life plans were not working. Grandpa set his coffee mug down and cleared his throat. "Well, what do you mean?" I think he knew what I was trying to say, but he used this as a teaching moment. I shrugged my shoulders and said, "I tried joining sports, changing my clothes, changing my personality, and every other aspect of who I am. I still ended up being an outsider in the end. What will *actually* work? How do I blend in with everybody else for good this time?"

He looked at me with a straight face and never skipped a beat. With 100% certainty, he said, "You don't hear how *stupid* that sounds, do you?" He put out his cigarette and lowered his eyebrows like John Wayne. He paused and held eye contact for a few seconds. I started gathering my thoughts to reply, but he beat me to the punch. "In five years, you are never going to see these people again. You might keep one or two good friends, but most of those people you're parading around with right now won't stick around. God gave you a gift, and here you are wasting it. It sure baffles me." He breathed out a puff of smoke and smirked. He threw his cigarette butt away and mumbled, "What you really

112

need are good friends, the kind that you can trust. It was pretty damn stupid to throw that away like you did." I shrugged my shoulders and said, "Well, they want nothing to do with me. I honestly get it. You don't know what I did." Grandpa pulled his suspenders and said, "I'm sure I don't...and I don't want to know! If you tell me, I'll probably just get ticked off, so save it for a priest. All I'm going to say is that life is short. Most of my old friends have passed away. Forty years felt like ten! If you don't try to fix things with Andrew and them, you will live with that regret for the rest of your life. The only reason they are hurting right now is because they still care! If you wait too long, they will move on from this and forget about you. That clock is ticking. You better ditch the pride and pity before the door slams in your face."

I dug around in the junk drawer and found the phone book. I looked up Andrew's phone number. I got nervous when I heard the dial tone. I was hoping his mom wouldn't be the one to answer. I felt too guilty and ashamed to talk to her. She was the type of person who did everything she could to help the needy. She wore her heart on her sleeve and a cross necklace around her neck. That's who she was; she was the textbook definition of a Christian woman. The fact that I successfully ticked her off spoke volumes. I had really messed up big time. The phone rang three times, and sure enough, it was her. I almost didn't have the stomach to speak. She could tell it was me by the guilt in my voice. I was riddled with shame. I was expecting the guilt trip of a lifetime. I thought she would tell me what a horrible person I had been. I assumed there would be nothing short of brimstone and fire. That's not what happened, though. She once again surprised me with her strong Christian attitude. The first words out of her mouth were, "Joey, are you doing okay?" I froze in shock. I told her that I was tired of living the way I was. I was finally ready to fix things.

I heard a door creaking in the background. "Andy, Joey's on the phone." To my surprise, his voice perked up. "Really, he is? Why did he call?" "I guess you'll have to find that out here." "Hey, Joey…" "Listen, Andy, I'm sorry. I've been a jackass for years, but you know what? I'm tired of living like this. I got good at acting like I had it all together, but I really didn't. This entire year was horrible. Those popular kids can be brutal! I guess you had a point. I can't really do anything I want and get away with it. I'm ready to start over, are you?"

I closed my eyes and nervously squeezed the phone. I could hear the static of a ceiling fan, so I knew he hadn't hung up. The anxiety was killing me. He finally broke the silence. "Joey, my momma raised me to be a Christian. That means I'm supposed to forgive. Do you know where we usually hang out at school? We're at the back table on the right. I hope I see you there tomorrow. I want to talk about this with the rest of the group."

I couldn't sleep that night. I grabbed a blanket and climbed on top of the camping trailer in our pasture. The A/C box was at just the right angle to be a pillow. It smelled very Earthy outside. The grass had just been cut. My shorts were getting stained white from the chalky roof paint. I looked at the sky and uttered, "What am I going to say tomorrow?" I tossed and turned up there, trying to come up with the perfect things to say. My mind went blank. A rooster woke me up from across the road. I snuck back into the house just before sunrise. I felt itchy all over. I went in and looked for decent clothes before taking a long shower.

I grabbed my sunglasses off the coat rack and headed for the door. Grandpa chugged down his coffee and zipped up the duffel bag. He saw me putting the sunglasses on and got a stern expression. He uttered in frustration, "Leave those stupid things here." I replied, "I don't want people to see the bags under my eyes!" He put one hand on his hip and pointed at me with the other. "I know your game. That's not why you're wearing them, and you know it. You're wearing the shades so you don't have to look those guys in the eye! If you want their respect, take the stupid things off. By the way, don't get clever and try to pull a fast one where you blame this mess on them. Unless they specifically ask you why you did something, keep that information to yourself. Excuses won't fix anything. When you apologize, you have to allow yourself to be vulnerable in order for it to mean anything. There's no way around that. Let God be the guide for what you say next, not your ego. Listen to understand, not just to respond. If you follow those three rules, it will be damn near impossible to mess up." I set the sunglasses on the fireplace mantle and went back to my old wallet with no chain on it. I didn't want to look anything like my old cocky self when I saw them again.

The bus hissed to a halt at school. My old friends were sitting exactly where Andrew said they would be. I was dragging my feet. I still didn't know what I would say to them. I timidly walked in, looking down at the floor tiles. The guilt hit hard. I hugged Andy and sat down. The rest of the group was confused. One of them crossed his arms. "Joey, what are you doing here? I thought you'd be at the basketball table with your 'real friends,' talking crap like usual." I shrugged my shoulders and took my backpack off. "Well, so did I. Honestly, I'm tired of that. After I made an ass of myself, I finally figured out that those people never really cared about me. Not like y'all did, anyway. I had a lot of fans but no friends. I haven't had real friends in years. I need people that I can actually trust. I'm ready to start over. I'm sorry for all of that shit I pulled, I really am."

Andrew crossed his arms and tightened his lips. "Joey, do you know you cuss a lot?" I spoke a kneejerk response without thinking it through. I snapped back in all seriousness, "Oh shit, sorry!" The group rolled their eyes and started laughing. Andy blushed and said, "Uh, Joey, that's exactly what I was talking about." I caught myself and swallowed my pride. I put my hands on the table. "Okay, okay, sorry! I know I've got a lot of work to do, I get it. I haven't been a good guy for a while. Are you at least willing to give me a second chance? It is much harder for bullies to go after someone when they are in a group. That means I can actually help you and vice versa. Besides that, I miss the old days! This is the longest meaningful conversation I have had in a long time." Andy shook his head. "I don't know about y'all, but I'm in. I'll give him a chance. I miss how it used to be before everything happened. Don't you guys miss that too?" The rest reluctantly agreed.

Hanging with my old friends started slowly knocking the "popular kid" habits out of me. Little by little, I started cussing less and being less snarky-spirited and less sarcastic too. It was the social reset that I desperately needed. I started a new way of life from scratch. When I gossiped about people, my friends called me out on it. I casually told them a story I had heard about a former teammate. Before I finished the story, Andrew said, "Do you know this for sure?" I shrugged and said, "Well, no, but I heard it from somebody else. I'm pretty sure it's legit." He put his hands together and replied, "Why are you saying it then, if you're not sure?" I smiled and put my hands up before giving it a rest. My friends had a major influence on me and helped me change my ways. One day they all came to school wearing T-shirts that said "Winter Jam" on them. Andy could not stop talking about it. He explained it to me. "Winter Jam is a Christian concert tour. You should go with us. It's a really powerful experience." I wasn't easily convinced, but I did eventually go. I wanted to see what all the fuss was about. What else did I have to do with my spare time?

We met early in the morning on Saturday to go to the concert. The first thing I did when I saw Andy's mom was to thank her for giving me that second chance. I knew that she had a major influence on the decision to forgive me; I could feel it. The boys took a restroom break as we headed to the stadium line. I finally spoke up. "I don't want to look a gift horse in the mouth here, but I never understood why you and the guys were so quick to forgive me. I probably wouldn't have let it go if I was on the other side. I was expecting that phone call to go very differently." Without skipping a beat, she had a response. "Well, our pastor taught us that if we want our own sins to be forgiven, then we need to forgive other people. Jesus forgave the people that persecuted him, so surely, we can forgive others for a lot less." I didn't know what to make of that; I had no response. I thought to myself, "Good for her, I suppose. If it were me, I would've ripped me a new one."

There were at least ten thousand people at the arena for Winter Jam. We got seats about halfway up the bleachers. A minister came on stage and told some stories that were even more profound than mine. They showed tweets on the big screen that were sent in by the crowd. The testimonies were endless. They made my struggles look like child's play by comparison. These stories really put things into perspective for me.

One of the lead bands was called Building 429. I had no clue who they were. They got their equipment set up while the lead singer hyped up the crowd. Their drummer gave the thumbs up and got ready. They started their gig with one of their biggest hits, "Where I Belong." The crowd went silent in anticipation. Cell phone flashlights were waving all over the stadium. It looked like the night sky. The opening lyrics were, "Sometimes it feels like I'm watching from the outside." My eyes opened wider, and I paid closer attention. His voice continued, "I won't keep searching for answers that aren't here to find." They had my undivided attention. The place exploded with energy as the chorus started. It was so loud that I could feel the reverberations in my chest.

It was a moving experience, but it didn't feel like I was in a church. I witnessed something that was more powerful than I had ever imagined. I started living for something bigger than my autism that night. My root desires were starting to change. I had new priorities. Perhaps what I wanted wasn't what I needed. I thought I knew what happiness was before this, but I didn't have a clue. I went back to my church and started taking my faith seriously. I unfollowed people on social media who were bad influences. I also started reading the Bible when I had the time. As I got away from my old life and closer to God, I developed a stronger conviction about right and wrong. When I did what was right, I felt a comforting warmth inside. When I did something wrong, I started feeling emotionally and physically uncomfortable. Telling lies or cursing caused my stomach to feel like it was tied in knots. Derogatory jokes stopped being funny. I didn't enjoy those things anymore. I could feel the Holy Spirit working on me. My eyes were opened to what God could offer me. I realized that I didn't have to return to my old way of living; I never wanted to go back to it.

Later that week, I had a strange request for Grandma. We were driving home from town. I said, "Do you mind stopping at a house right off the highway up here? There's something I need to do." She agreed and didn't ask any questions. We pulled up a long driveway. It was the home of a guy whom I had picked on for a long time. Grandma was unaware of this part of my life. She stopped the car, and I moseyed up to a screen door. The guy I was looking for saw me and walked outside. He crossed his arms and looked at me sternly. I honestly understood why. I did my best to look up at him. "Listen, I feel a lot of guilt weighing on my heart, and I had to stop here to tell you something. I'm sorry for what I did to you all those years. Please know that it had nothing to do with you; it had to do with me. I really wish I could undo that stuff, but I can't. I'm done picking on people. I've had enough of that life. If you're ever looking for a table to sit at, look for my group." He put his hands in his pockets, looked down at the ground, and asked, "Well, what about those lies you told your friends about me? Do they still believe them?" I sighed and said, "Not for much longer. I intend to set the record straight. You don't need to be afraid of me anymore." I saw him in the cafeteria the next week and motioned for him to join our group. This guy whom I used to bully gradually became one of my closest friends.

I went home and tried on my basketball team hoodie for old times' sake. I quickly realized it was too tight to fit. I took it off and tossed it into the Goodwill box in the kitchen. Grandma was donating the box to less fortunate kids. It didn't bother me to see it go. A year earlier, it would have been unthinkable. I practically worshipped the dang thing at one point. I wasn't that same guy anymore. The hoodie was gone, but I kept the team backpack. I hung it up in my home office. I put it there partly for nostalgia, but not entirely. That black-and-gold bag collecting dust was a physical reminder of who I used to be. It gave me a point of reference. My middle school career taught me what not to do with my life. I had no business chasing those girls I was going after, or manipulating everyone into thinking of me exactly how I wanted them to. I hated the anxiety and regret that my old lifestyle forced me to carry. I promised myself that I'd never compromise my integrity to be popular again.

CHAPTER THIRTEEN — Team Sport

I n high school, Thursday was the day my friends and I walked across the town park. We were going to a gas station called Granny's Fried Chicken. This was what most high-schoolers did if they didn't have their driver's license yet. If the wind blew just right, we could faintly smell it from the parking lot. We couldn't resist. The line to get in wrapped around the building, sometimes into the street. Two packs of people made the mile-long walk every day. The lead pack consisted of the teacher's pets who got out of class early. This included the jocks, the cheerleaders, and the teacher's aides. The second pack was the largest one. We were sprinkled somewhere in the middle.

There was a girl sitting on the sidewalk when we returned to campus one Thursday. She had glasses and headphones on. A group of people wearing camo jackets surrounded her. They kicked her belongings around. She exclaimed to them, "Leave me alone! What do you want?" They slowly paced backward and started calling her horrible names. One person said, "Nobody wants you anyway! You're going to die alone!" They laughed at her and kept walking. I couldn't keep my mouth shut. Those people ticked me off. I aggressively shouted at them, "Was that really necessary?" They rolled their eyes and yelled back, "You clearly don't know her." I told my friends I needed to make a pit stop at the restroom, and I would catch up with them. They took off, and I walked over to the girl's spot. She didn't talk much, but she did smile at me. She said, "I appreciate what you're trying to do, but it's a losing battle. I'm honestly used to it at this point."

She asked me why I took that chance, standing up to the bullies. I shrugged my shoulders. "I always wished someone would do that for me, but they never did. I don't know...it just felt like the right thing to do." I did the best I could to turn her frown into a smile when the opportunity came. I made it a habit to stop and visit with her every Thursday for five minutes, then go catch up with the guys. This went on for a month or two. She finally became comfortable enough to take the headphones off. She started talking to me more. She eventually got the courage to invite herself to walk to Granny's Fried Chicken with us. She introduced herself to us as Charlotte. For some strange reason, I remembered that name from somewhere. I couldn't put my finger on it, but I knew for a fact I had seen that name somewhere before.

Something clicked. I suddenly remembered where I had seen her name. I looked through a yearbook and confirmed my suspicions. She was the same girl who wrote me a note way back in middle school. I had made fun of her at the time and didn't even realize who it was. She had walked past and heard everything I said. I didn't know what to do with that information, so I chose not to mention it. I was hoping to avoid an awkward conversation.

She joined our pack, and it started off innocently. I didn't feel a need or desire to impress her, so I wasn't nervous. I had my eye on someone else at the time, and so did she. Gradually, things changed. She started dressing nice and hanging around longer. She became bolder and more confident. I had never seen her act like that. Her actions caught me off-guard. She could talk my ear off and even knew how to make me laugh. That last part was a tall order back then. I never intended to fall for her. I dismissed it as nothing more than hormones. I assumed it would fade away in a week or so. I didn't want to risk saying something stupid, so I closed that door in my mind.

My friends saw the signs, but I didn't pick up on them. Everyone could tell that she was flirting, except for me. She asked what I thought of the week's NASCAR race. I ranted about the storylines from the race, not having a clue. "Who's your favorite driver?" She looked blindsided by the question. She made a steering wheel gesture. She pretended to swerve into me and said, "Don't you think I'd make a good racecar driver?" Her eyes were on me as she bit her lip. This may have been obvious flirting to most people but not to me. I killed the moment by replying, "I don't know, you need to have a lot of sponsors. It costs about two or three hundred grand to race. It's pretty difficult to learn how to drive all of the racetracks." She sighed and laughed before taking off to class. My friends rolled their eyes and said, "Joey, you know what she was doing, right?" I thought my friends were yanking my chain.

She had to make it painfully obvious for me to connect the dots. I finally came out and said, "You should probably know what you're getting into. I'm not a big-time star anymore. I haven't even been asked to sign an autograph in years! If you're looking for fame, you're going to be disappointed. I'm not that guy anymore." She smiled and said, "I know. That's why I'm giving you a chance." I was quite surprised she said this, considering the way I had talked about her all those years ago. When we made it official, it took me a while to look at her as the girlfriend. It was a huge transition with a lot of unknowns. I had no clue what I was doing.

She came out of class darting her eyes one day. She was fidgeting and stuttering over her words. Something was clearly not right. I pulled her hair back and asked, "So, do you want to talk about it?" She gave a high-pitched laugh and looked at me with contempt. "Uh, what?" I shrugged my shoulders. "Well...I don't really know. Whatever is bothering you." She gave me a tight-lipped smile and raised her hands. She exclaimed, "I'm fine!" This was quite confusing because I could tell by her demeanor that she was not fine. I looked at the situation from a purely logical perspective. I pressed on, asking for details. I was trying to collect enough information to comprehend where her emotional reaction was coming from. Most people would have known that being told that she was "fine" was a signal to put a pin in that conversation. I did not know about this unspoken social rule. My intent was good, but my intentions were not viewed as relevant. Eventually, she got mad and uttered in frustration, "What I mean is, I don't want to talk about it anymore!" My eyebrows raised as the epiphany finally hit me. I simply replied, "Oh, there's nothing wrong with that. Why didn't you just say this? It was not clear." The only response I got was, "Because that's not what people do! Ugh!"

I knew I had to tell her the truth about me. It seemed like the right thing to do before she got too emotionally attached. Later that day, she sat down as usual. I sat with her for a good thirty seconds before I finally said, "There is something you should know about me before this goes any further." She eyeballed me up and down very nervously. It got very awkward, very quickly. "O...kay, what?" I took a deep breath. "Remember how I couldn't read between the lines when you said you were fine? I misinterpret a lot of social cues. That is pretty much the story of my life. I have a condition called Asperger Syndrome; it is a form of autism. I don't automatically know things that I'm 'supposed to.' You're going to have to be a little patient with me if you want this to work. I think you should research what Asperger Syndrome is and get back to me. If you lose interest in me afterward, I get it. I need a really special girl in my life who can handle this." She sighed with relief and put her hand on her chest. "Jeez, of course, I know what autism is. I know lots of people like that! Don't scare me like that over nothing!" I threw my head back in amusement. My eyebrows raised. "Nothing? I thought you would instantly dump me when I told you that. Most girls I know seem to only want loud, cocky guys. The crazy part is that those same guys end up treating them horribly. They won't give introverted guys like me a chance! I've never understood that, but I guess that's just how it is." She rolled her eyes and chuckled back, "Well, not all of us are like that. Boy, you definitely have a lot to learn!" The fact that she stuck around after the disclaimer spoke volumes to me.

She was the first girl I knew who didn't judge me for being autistic. She didn't treat me like I had less dignity than other guys. In her eyes, I wasn't damaged goods. She never tried to pressure me to act more "normal." She rarely complained about my learning process. Most of what I knew about relationships and dating, I learned from her. She told me things that most girls were simply not willing to tell their significant other. She never used that against me. We were abnormally honest with each other. She didn't put me down behind my back; she did the opposite. She stood up for me. I knew how rare this was and didn't intend to waste it. I treated her the best I could, given my limited knowledge.

The relationship was unconventional by our peers' standards, but it worked. She stood up for me when no one else would. She was my biggest fan. It wasn't long before I hung with her more than anybody else. We ate a lot of gas station chicken and listened to way too much Shawn Mendes. Seriously, I just about needed "stitches" after listening to that song so many times. I eventually wised up and invested in headphones of my own.

In the morning, I was usually the first one on her bus. We headed down to the dirt roads. Seats started filling up as we approached her stop. She got on with a somber face. She hugged me and grabbed her headphones. She looked terrified. I asked her what was going on. "I can't stand these people that are about to get on. You'll see why."

We stopped at a trailer park. There was a group of ten or so. They all hopped on and went to the back. They were dropping all kinds of vulgar language. The little kids talked like sailors too. There was constant fighting, screaming, and bullying. They had zero respect for anybody. I had never seen a group of people act so hatefully. I got a glimpse into a world I had never seen before. I started understanding where she was coming from. They treated us both horribly. We were targets. The odds were not in our favor.

Several people crowded around our seats. One of them bounced a tennis ball off the window. A girl looked at us and said, "Both of you are retards." The whole bunch laughed like drunken hyenas. Charlotte's ears turned red. She was about to lose it and go off on them. I put my hand on the seatback and did my best to talk her down. I told her to trust me for a second.

I tried something that was out of my comfort zone. I boldly said, "Hold on, explain it to me. I don't get it yet." The girl rolled her eyes and quietly said, "See? You are a retard!" I leaned closer and asked her to repeat it. She said it louder this time. I stayed calm and said, "What exactly do you mean by that?" I got her to repeat it yet again. When she said it the third time, her friends' smiles mellowed and turned into blank faces. The laughter quickly stopped. They paused and stared at her awkwardly. The joke was getting old. She looked around and tried to get it going again. She yanked her friend's hair and said, "Come on, doesn't anybody agree with me? I mean, look at them!" Her friends made stern expressions and slapped her hand away. They said, "Don't freaking touch my hair!" They got annoyed with her and shrugged it all off. It wasn't funny to them anymore. The moment had passed. Nobody was laughing. She exasperated in frustration and flicked her hair.

She crossed her arms and looked back at me. She said, "What the hell are you smiling at, freak-face?" I smiled back and said, "Notice how your pals aren't laughing?" She got mad and said in a snappy voice, "What are you talking about?" With no hesitation, I cleared my throat and put my hand on my chin. I said, "If you're so smart, then you can figure it out! How did I get them to stop laughing?" She puckered her lips and scrunched her nose. She did not have an answer. She shrugged and uttered, "I don't freaking know... eye contact or something?" I raised my eyebrows and said, "You don't look so smart now, do you? You're the one on academic probation, not us. We don't have to give up our lunchtimes to go to tutoring every day. We are both passing in all classes. You can't say the same. Who is the real smart one here?" She started gathering her thoughts to escalate further.

"I'll tell you what, if you apologize and take back what you said, I'll retract my end. I'm open to compromise if you are." She reluctantly agreed. A few minutes later, she randomly turned around out of nowhere. "So, what kind of stupid-ass mind trickery did you use anyway?" I gleefully replied, "I never agreed to tell you that. This wasn't part of the deal."

Charlotte asked me about this incident later in the week. We were walking back to the high school from the gas station. We had to hurry because it was starting to thunder and we saw lightning bolts in the distance. She hunched her shoulders and complained that she was cold. I gave her my jacket and pulled the hood up. She hugged me and hysterically said, "That's not exactly what I meant!" She laughed and put her hands in the pockets. "Oh sweet, free gum! Thanks!"

She put her drink in my bag. She cleared her throat. "I don't know how you got that terrible witch to back down on the bus, but props! You're going to have to teach me how you pulled that off." I finally did. "So, my Grandpa took psychology classes in college. He told me that if you get someone to repeat their joke three times, they usually stop laughing. It's annoying when you ask them to explain it to you. They don't like it because it messes up the dynamic. They want you to get angry and defend yourself. That's the fun part for them! After they explain themselves three times, it's not as funny anymore. There's something about repetition that people just don't like in social situations. You've got to keep your cool in order for this trick to work."

She was suddenly amused. She pressed her lips together to keep herself from laughing. "I think it's ironic that you understand that type of psychology, but you had no clue what I meant back there." I thought about it but still didn't know. I replied, "Well, you said you were cold, and I had a jacket in my bag, so it all worked out. What hidden meaning could there be to that?" She laughed out loud and said, "Well, I wasn't really that cold. I was hoping you would hold me! Girls say that they're cold for all kinds of reasons." I mumbled back, "That is so confusing. I'm really doing the best I can." She smiled and laid her head on my shoulder. "I know, thanks for at least being a good sport about it. Sorry if I sounded snappy; that wasn't my intent." "Well, for what it's worth, I'll get the hang of this eventually." She shook her head and laughed again. "Um, you won't understand girls 100%, but that's okay! That's not an autism thing, that's just a guy thing. I would say that the majority of guys misinterpret what girls do. It's not just you. Quit being so hard on yourself. We can be very complicated creatures."

Another girl was hanging out at our lunch table when I got there. She messed up Charlotte's ponytail and grabbed food off her tray. Charlotte's jaw was clenched. Her eyes were wide open. She looked like a coiled viper snake about to strike. She was clearly not happy. The other girl smiled at me and patted Charlotte's back. "Hey, there's your boy! I guess we're about to find that out, aren't we?" She hunched over and said, "I bet I can steal him from you." I snapped back, "N...no, you can't. I wouldn't do that to her. Besides, even if I weren't taken, I still wouldn't be attracted to you. We don't have that type of connection. It's nothing personal, so please don't take it that way. This is a big school with plenty of guys for you to choose from. Best of luck to you." She leaned over the table in a way where I could see down her shirt. She said in a soft voice, "Yes, it is personal, and yes, I can. Charlotte is pissing me off. I'm going to get her back. Just watch me." She looked up at me through her eyelashes. I rolled my eyes and replied, "Please leave. I'm asking as nicely as I can." She smirked as she left. I mumbled, "Who does she think she is? People are unbelievable!"

The next semester, that girl and I had a class together. She sat next to me and tried to talk bad about Charlotte. I was told to stay out of it for the time being. I ignored the girl and tried to keep the peace. On one occasion, she tried aggressively to talk me into leaving Charlotte. She told me that Charlotte was unpopular and that I should try to get a more popular girl. I finally got fed up enough to speak out. "I've tried being nice to you, but you're clearly not getting this. I don't give a rip about popularity. I haven't cared about it since eighth grade. There is nothing less attractive to me than a girl who's full of herself. It is repulsive when someone thinks their crap doesn't stink. That's why I don't want anything to do with people like you. I've already been there and done that. I have sold out my friends for fame before, and I'm not making that mistake again! I'm not afraid of people like you anymore. If you pick on her again and I see it, I will not be this nice next time. I will call you out publicly and make a big scene! It won't be pretty. That's not a threat, that's a promise. Leave her alone."

I went on with my day and forgot about this encounter. I set my binders next to the classroom door and left. I walked out front and waited for Charlotte. I helped lift her bags into her locker and patted my pockets to make sure I hadn't forgotten my spending money. She looked as if she was about to cry. She gave a half-smile and exclaimed, "I heard about what you did." My heart nearly skipped a beat. I didn't know what she was referring to. "I'm not sure how to react yet. I need more information first." She bear-hugged me and said, "Thank you so much for sticking up for me. I really appreciate that. Someone told me what you said to that girl. You really meant all of that, didn't you?"

I started to organize my thoughts to respond, but she beat me to it. She hugged me tighter and wouldn't let me get away. "I'm going to return the favor. If they start coming after you for this, please tell me about it. If anybody messes with you, there will be hell to pay! I am so done with bullies! It stops right now. I deserve to be treated with respect, and so do you. We're going to beat this crap!" I had never agreed with anything more in my life.

This battle cry began a two-year-long journey. We fought back and conquered the high school world. We teamed up and took on the bullies. Her bullies were my bullies too. We really were a team. She helped me get through high school in more ways than one. She kept her promise, even though I had a hard time keeping mine on some occasions.

Charlotte came around the corner to join the boys and me one day. Shortly afterward, the noon bell rang. People on academic probation were being released. A guy swaggered out of the hallway. He turned in our direction with excitement. Andrew began stuttering over his words and looking around. He hunched over and rubbed his eyes. "Oh great, it's him." I looked over and saw nothing out of the ordinary. "What are you talking about?" Andy shrugged and whispered, "Just give it a second, watch." The guy came toward our group and nodded at me. I nodded back. He smirked and then suddenly charged at Andy as a prank. He messed up his hair and tried to snatch his iPad away with no success. Charlotte nudged me and whispered, "Aren't you going to do something?"

I saw the bully's face and froze. I sat there for a few more seconds while I debated it in my head. I didn't know what would happen to me if I spoke up. I stuck my arm out to block his path. He stopped and lowered his eyebrows in confusion. "What are you doing, bro?" My heart started thumping. My whole body wanted to stay silent, but I fought against it. I loudly said, "are you sure you want to do that in front of me?" I sighed and stood up. I slowly inched toward him. He backed up. Against my better judgment, I kept advancing. I exclaimed, "I've had enough. BACK...UP!"

There was an awkward silence afterward. Several people put their hands over their mouths and got bug-eyed. The bully looked around and yelled, "What are your dumbasses looking at?" I waved to get his attention. "If you leave them alone, it all stops here. If you force me to fight back, I will not fight fair. Think this through. You are far outnumbered." He breathed fast and scrunched his nose. "You just better watch your back, Joey..." He jabbed his finger in my face. Charlotte stood up and helped me out. "You better leave him the hell alone, too. If anything happens to him, I will show you just how crazy I can be. You're going to see a side of me you've never seen before!" I looked at her face and felt a cold chill run down my spine. She looked like a boxer about to go into the ring. I had never seen that look before. I couldn't help but proudly smile at her as the bully stormed off. He exclaimed, "You're both crazy!" I mumbled, "I'm glad you think that! Keep thinking it."

From that day forward, we made it more difficult for bullies. When I saw them in action, I announced their full names so that everyone could hear them. I wasn't scared of them anymore. Their threats meant nothing to me. When I stood up for what was right, I noticed that other people helped me. Several people stood up to bullies and joined the fight. My faith grew deeper in God's ability to conquer this. I found refuge in that and took a bolder stand. I became a more assertive person than I had ever been. I declared war on bullying and started seeing results. A school-wide movement began to form. They all decided that bullying was old news. We took all of the fun out of it for them.

The bullies moved on to their next targets and finally left us alone. The majority would eventually win the war.

CHAPTER FOURTEEN — Renewed Purpose

I saw my middle school art teacher in town one day. He asked me if I was still drawing. I didn't want to lie to him. I replied, "Not really. It's been a busy couple of years." He replied, "Hmm, that's a slippery slope. Several people quit creating and lost their knack for it. I think that's a real shame. Have you considered the AP art program at the high school? You'd probably do great in there." "Yeah, I agree! I did good in Art 1. I can't get into the AP class until I'm a junior. I'm just waiting it out." He smiled and swiped his hand. "Ah, that's nonsense! They make exceptions all the time! I can talk to some people." I felt something tugging on my heart, but I ignored it.

Charlotte and I went to a movie theater in the mall. There were several movie posters on the wall that appeared to be hand-drawn. We both looked at them while we waited in line at the concession stand. "Why did you quit drawing, Joey?" I shrugged it off and watched the cars go by outside. Charlotte waved her hand over my face to get my attention. "Wait, what?" She exclaimed, "I said, why did you stop drawing?" I winked at her and held her hand. I eyeballed her up and down and pulled her close. "Well, I've been too busy. It's not a big deal." She yanked her hand away and raised both in the air. "Yes, it is a big deal, Joey! I don't want you to quit your passion because of me. That's not okay!" I rolled my eyes in exasperation. "I thought I was the one who missed all the social cues! I am obviously just flirting. You really didn't pick up on it?" She rolled her eyes. "Yeah, yeah. Now is not the time!" She leaned closer. "Tell me the real reason you quit." I shook my head. "Well, my art career has been stagnant for months. I haven't gotten any client commissions, and it isn't taking off like I thought it would. Maybe this entrepreneurship thing isn't for me. I don't really know." I was starting to question if I would make it as an artist. I thought about giving up on my art and switching to a steadier career.

She took a deep breath and patted me on the back. She said, "Well, dang. That's too bad, I really liked you." "Wait, what is that supposed to mean?" She zipped up her jacket and put her hair down. "I don't date quitters. No girl likes a guy with that attitude." I smirked and said, "Very funny. You're bluffing." She crossed her arms and said, "Maybe I am, maybe I'm not. Are you willing to risk it? If you're going to quit on me, then I guess I'll have no choice but to quit on you. I can't stand in the way of a talent like yours. I'm not going to let you blame me for your dreams not coming true. That isn't how I roll. If you want your art to go big, you've got to take risks." I nodded my head with excitement. "Thanks. I really appreciate what you're trying to do. It is probably the push I need." I hugged her. She smelled incredible. I didn't want to leave, but I knew I had to. She pointed at the door and said, "What are you doing here? You know what you need to do. Go... Yeah, right now! Go! I'll have my mom pick me up when she's out of Walmart." She waved and smiled at me as I called a ride.

Nobody knew this, but she was the biggest cheerleader for my art career at that time. We often wore matching sprint car T-shirts that I got from clients. She went to the racetrack and did everything she could to support my art business. For a short time, she believed in my business more than I did.

I went to the office and filled out some paperwork the following week. I decided to start taking my art seriously. I started getting good at it again. My drawings changed dramatically. Before I knew it, I was sitting in the AP art room. I walked in and saw a class I had always dreamed of. It was an entire class period of just creating, nothing else. I thought this was going to be the easiest A-plus I had ever gotten. I sat in the back row with my head high and waited for the teacher. "Welcome to our little fortress. I will be your AP studio art instructor. This class can be a lot of fun, but it will push you out of your comfort zone. I'm just warning you about that up front." We were told to grab a sketchbook with our names on them. We had one big project due every two weeks and a sketch every Monday. At the beginning of every project, we presented a reference image and the art medium we were planning to use. It was up to the teacher to approve or disapprove of them.

I printed a bunch of NASCAR photographs and got ready for the easiest semester ever. When I got to the front of the room, that idea was shot out of the water. "Yeah...that's not happening. Let's start with a still-life." She pulled out a flower vase and handed it to me, along with a canvas. I rolled my eyes and mumbled, "You're kidding, right?" She set it on the table and replied, "Did I stutter?" Right then, I knew that this class was not going to be the cakewalk I had expected. She wasn't a blind fan like everyone else. I had to earn every ounce of respect that I got.

AP art class was the push I needed. I wasn't crazy about it at the time, but it gave me a deeper appreciation for the art world. I formed a deep respect for good painters, that's for sure. I realized just how difficult painting really is. It was an entirely different world. By the end of the second year, I was a completely different artist than I was in the beginning. I started building a portfolio, piece by piece. When I finally got compliments from the AP teacher, I knew I was doing something right.

I took my portfolio with me everywhere I went. People started taking notice. My reputation slowly changed among my peers. I gained their respect again. They treated me like an equal. Everyone cheered me on and supported my art talent. I finally had an identity that I could live with. This was the confirmation that I needed to pursue this as a legitimate career. So, that is exactly what I did.

I brought my portfolio to several NASCAR races. I was lucky enough to meet some renowned NASCAR drivers. I got them to sign artwork of themselves and their cars as an excuse to talk to them. My uncle was in the back of the crowd and managed to capture these moments on camera. The pictures were posted online, and the hype went crazy. These posts laid the stage for my social media presence. I began offering illustration and graphic design services. I posted time-lapse drawing videos to build public interest. The videos were very well received. Many people seemed to enjoy watching them, so they became my primary marketing platform. Once I gained some momentum, the social media algorithms started working in my favor. The number of shares started growing, and so did the view counts. My website became big enough to register as an official business.

I wanted to try my hand with some local drivers. I looked up local venues and racing organizations. I discovered a regional sprint car organization called the Oil Capital Racing Series. I found their email address and typed the best pitch for my illustration service I had ever typed. I edited it and edited it again. I finally clicked "Send" when I felt ready. I hoped for the best. A little while later, I got the call. I was invited to create illustrations for racers attending their awards banquet in Tulsa. I knew that this was an all-or-nothing moment. It was going to be my big break.

I was greeted by their public relations director. The plan was to raffle off two of my original illustrations. I handed over the art pieces and went in to find my family's table. I was excited to see where the night could lead. I felt good about it. I created brochures for my new art business and placed them at each table. The announcer, John, proceeded to give the season's awards. My art pieces were displayed along the front edge of the stage. John picked up the microphone and introduced the idea of a raffle to the crowd. I saw some attendees trying to get his attention. They whispered something to him. He nodded his head and announced that it was now up for auction at the audience's request. He said my name and asked me to come up to the stage. I was excited but also terrified. I was not prepared to speak in front of a crowd. I didn't have a chance to practice; I had no idea what I would say. I was very nervous about the idea of winging it. I reluctantly went up there.

My heart was pounding. I didn't want to talk too much, but I also needed to talk about the pieces. I knew how powerful word of mouth was. I looked straight at my family to keep my composure. Looking at one person was much less intimidating than looking around at the whole crowd. I framed it like a conversation with one person. I was asked some tough questions that I didn't know how to answer, but I tried to react the same way I would if it was just my family in there.

I never thought the auction would go the way it did. The bidding kept getting higher and higher. I was in a state of shock. I didn't even know what to say to the auction winner; I was speechless. My profits that night made it possible to buy my first truck. I took great pride in my Silverado, knowing the people in that room made it happen for me. I greatly appreciated the OCRS teams and promoters for giving that big break to an unknown, unproven 15-year-old. John became one of my best friends and mentors. I remember him saying that I was genuinely different from most people he knew in my age group. That was one of the most heartfelt compliments I ever got. I did the best I could to live up to that bar he set for me.

Now, I knew with 100% confidence that a creative career was in my future. When fall came, I enrolled in graphic design at the Technology Center. It was a big learning curve. It required a great deal of hard work. I put in the work to make it and was rewarded an internship with a local, family-owned T-shirt printing company. The owner was a very knowledgeable man who taught me almost everything I know about digital illustration. I also learned how a design goes from a computer screen to a shirt and everything in between. That family was incredible to work for. I liked working there so much that I stayed through most of the summer and came back occasionally when I had the time. I hope I am lucky enough to work for a creative director like them for a living.

My art career started to take off during junior year. Everyone respected my art. My choice to stay with Charlotte, on the other hand, did not go as well as I had hoped. I got teased often about my relationship with her. Eyes rolled at the mention of her name. I fought to maintain this relationship as hard as I could. She had been there since the beginning. She had been my inspiration. Standing up for each other was the foundation of our relationship but was that enough?

It got difficult for me and Charlotte to see each other. Her parents were upset after learning that she had a boyfriend. The principal ordered us to stay away from each other at their request. We all know that telling teenagers to stay away from each other is not a smart thing to do; that wasn't going to happen. We started to sneak around. I felt like I was living in a thriller movie with my partner in crime. We were on and off again for a long time. We kept standing up for each other the whole time, even when we weren't in the same room. The stresses of sneaking around and knowing that her parents disapproved only put more strain on the relationship.

As we grew older, the battles were becoming less and less frequent. Drama was a rare occurrence. Our peers finally learned to tolerate us. We overcame the bullying. When we did, we lost something in the process. Our common goal was gone. Now that we had nothing to fight for, we were forced to look at ourselves in the mirror. That was when it became clear that we wanted different things in life. She often became uncomfortable with me expressing my religious beliefs. I gradually stopped opening up about my Christian values to avoid arguments. This drove a wedge between us. I quickly learned that we disagreed on many other things, as well. It got to a point where we disagreed more than we agreed. I felt the distance becoming wider, and I knew that I was beginning to lose her. As clichéd as it sounds, we honestly grew apart. The purpose of our time together had been fulfilled. That chapter of our lives was ending. She began showing romantic interest in other people, and my eyes started to wander also. When I noticed this, I knew it was a done deal. We had to quit trying to change each other and let the relationship come to an end.

Our peers followed us around campus like paparazzi after we split up. Everything was fair game for public ridicule; it was a rough few weeks. She did what she felt was necessary to take care of herself. When she chose to berate me, I said very little in return. I knew the gossip would burn out if I didn't add to it; I needed to starve the fire. Because of her, I had the strength to wait out the storm. Eventually, the ranting stopped. She moved on, and so did I. Our relationship finally became old news.

Later, several people questioned the wisdom of my choice to date Charlotte. Grandma said that she thought Charlotte was trouble from the very start. My friends asked me what I was thinking. Her parents weren't big fans of me, and my folks weren't big fans of her. Our teachers also rolled their eyes. Despite how it ended, I never regretted dating Charlotte. She helped me overcome bullying. She was the motivation that I needed to stand up to my fears. I wouldn't have done it without her. I was perfectly content with letting the bullies win until I met her. I simply accepted that bullying would always be a part of my life. After those two years, I gained way too much self-respect to think that way anymore. The bar was raised for my future relationships and career. I hope that I was also able to help her in some way.

CHAPTER FIFTEEN — True Freedom

I left the art room and sat my bag down in my next class. The lights were dim, but I could see a person's silhouette at the end of the hall. I was walking out when I heard, "Joey, that's you, right?" I smirked and exclaimed, "That depends. Who's asking?" I never heard a response. Whoever it was, went out the door. I didn't think anything of it. I went out shortly afterward. I turned the corner and immediately knew who it was.

A former bully had moved back to town. I hadn't seen him since eighth grade. Now it was senior year, and I had almost forgotten about him. The sight of Braxton's face brought back memories that I hoped would never resurface. Everything he said and did suddenly flooded my mind. He slowly looked up at me. "Joey, I need to talk to you." The memories were so vivid that I interrupted him and backed away. "I still remember what you did. Why should I give you the time of day?" He shrugged his shoulders and said, "That's what I want to talk to you about." I cut him off again. "Yeah, well, you are a total bastard. Remember when you and the others punched me for no reason? How about that time you had the audacity to tell me that I should go kill myself? Do you seriously expect me to just forget something like that? You don't deserve the air you breathe!" I raised my hands as I stormed off, whispering, "Un-freaking-believable!"

I got away from him as quickly as I could. I mumbled under my breath, "I HATE that guy!" Sadly, I truly meant it down to my bones. I felt a wave of vengeful heat cascade through my body. My fists were clinched tightly enough to snap a pencil in two. The blood vessels felt like they would pop out of my head. Every time I replayed those memories, I got more worked up. It seemed so unfair. I had to put up with relentless bullying from him, and now he wanted to get away with all of it. I briskly walked through the parking lot to catch up with the boys.

"Who was that, Joey?" "A guy who deserves to go to hell, that's who! He will fit right in!" My friends were all taken aback. They did not see this coming. "Jeez, Joey! You're usually a level-headed dude. I don't know about you, but I don't hate anybody bad enough to wish hell on them. That is a whole other level, man. What did he do?" I shrugged. "You know what, I probably shouldn't say. If I tell you, you will hate that guy even more than I do. It's all right, though. He's going to mess with someone much bigger than he is one day, and it will go really bad. He'll be in a wheelchair for the rest of his life. I won't feel an ounce of remorse when it happens to him." I looked away so my friends wouldn't catch me smiling about it. I didn't want to look like a psychopath. I knew in my heart that feeling this way was wrong, but the hurt was still there.

I went to Great-Grandma's place on Saturday like always. I found an old door at the edge of the pasture. This was sort of a family dump for old worn-out things. It was a hollow wooden door that had been eaten by bugs, weather, and the elements. It was barely staying together. I rolled up my sleeves and grabbed a couple of things. I got a Sharpie, a cigarette lighter, and a bucket. I dragged the door out to the pasture and then to an abandoned gravel driveway in the woods. The family dump had tires, mattresses, old appliances, and rusty car parts everywhere. I propped the door up between a couple of loose branches. I set the bucket down and grabbed the Sharpie. I drew small ovals. These ovals represented the bullies' faces. I went to the pond to get a full bucket of water. Before I set the door on fire, I punched it with everything I had. When my fist got tired and numb, I threw rusty tools and hammers at it. I started throwing everything that I could get my hands on. I wore myself out. My back and sides were killing me. I was wheezing and coughing from exhaustion.

I grabbed some dried grass from the pasture and stuffed it into the hole at the base of the door. I set the grass on fire and watched it consume the door. It felt good to watch it burn. The Sharpie ink got darker as the wood turned black. The whole door was hissing. It almost sounded like the bullies screaming for help. I crossed my arms and mumbled, "How do YOU like torture? I can't wait till the day comes that you all burn for what you did." My teeth clenched with anger. I couldn't tell if I was feeling the heat of the fire or just the rage inside of me. Either way, my sides and back were soaked with sweat. I squeezed my shirt and watched the sweat drip onto the ground. There was an hour of daylight left, which meant it was about six o'clock. The food Grandma had been cooking was probably ready. I grabbed the water bucket to douse the fire. My arms felt wobbly. I walked closer and dumped most of it. The flames went out, and the door crackled. I kicked it over to make sure I hadn't missed any flames on the other side. The whole thing broke into tiny chunks. The smoke ceased, so I thought the fire was over. I poured the rest of the water over my legs and shoes to cool them off.

I started to walk back to the house when I noticed a flickering light. A small patch of grass had started burning in the middle of the driveway. It was spreading very slowly. I stomped on it and put it back out. I thought it was surely safe to leave this time, but the grass lit again. I had to make a second trip to the pond before it finally went out for good. The food was cold by the time I got back in the house. People were washing the dishes and cleaning up. I had to hurry. I realized that I had wasted the whole evening. That was a lot of work, just for a brief moment of satisfaction. A tiny bit of glee was not worth all of the effort I put into it.

The bitterness stayed with me for a long time. The weight on my shoulders got heavier the longer I carried it. These guys were still at school every day. I had to be around them even when I tried to avoid them. When I was forced to face them, I found myself fantasizing about the snarky remarks I could have made. I wanted to make them feel guilty and ashamed of themselves. I could never come up with the perfect remark to say, so I never spoke up. My entire worldview began to change. The anger was taking over other areas of my life. I quickly became a very pessimistic person.

Once, I started to roll out of the high school parking lot in my truck when I saw a face that was all too familiar. He walked right in front of me and strutted ridiculously slowly. He was walking as if he owned the place. He stopped and smirked at me. He put his hands up and stuck his tongue out. That was the final straw. I revved my engine to scare him. He flinched and ran out of the way. His friends laughed. I turned the radio up loud and shook my head. I mumbled, "You're lucky I'm too chicken to actually do it!"

I was so mad about it all that I just needed to get out of there. There was a long line of cars on the highway. I tailgated the van in front of me and then went for it. It was a freshly paved stretch with cornfields on both sides. There were no hills and only a few trees. I had half a mile, but it was a long line; I passed five or six cars. Suddenly, an SUV pulled out from a side road into the oncoming lane. I thought I still had time, so I pushed the pedal to the floor. I drove so fast that I hit the rev limiter. The engine made sounds that I had never heard before. It was knocking like an old clothes dryer. I felt the steering wheel shutter, and then the power began cutting out. I began to doubt if I was going to make it. I heard the tires squealing as I yanked it back into the lane. I barely made it with half a second to spare. The rear end fishtailed. My heart was racing much faster than the truck was. I looked down at the speedometer and realized how fast I was going. I came to my senses and let off the throttle. As I coasted, my emotions cooled off. That stunt I pulled because of my anger could have killed me. My heart felt very grateful inside. I looked up at the clouds on the horizon and uttered, "Thanks. I get it, I get it." I parked in the garage at home. It did not smell good. The next day, it wouldn't start. That is when I realized that the anger was beginning to control me, and not in a good way.

I shook my head when I passed by Braxton in the hall. I thought to myself, "Just look at him! Look at what he did. Sick bastards like him never change." I pushed the classroom door. As I turned the doorknob, it flew open. I could feel myself starting to fall. It wasn't possible for me to grab the doorframe in time. I nearly fell right on my face. I barely caught myself. The room was empty. Luckily, nobody saw me. I got up and wiped the dirt off my jeans. That is when I felt something thump inside my head. I heard a voice in the background. "You sure are one to talk! You need to let go. You can't keep living like this." I looked around, and no one was there. I realized that it was a Higher Power trying to get my attention. Initially, I shrugged it off. I figured there was no way God would ask me to do something so ridiculous. I was not ready to listen. The hatred in my heart for bullies was too strong. I wanted justice to be served. It seemed like the only way to move forward.

Grandma got my truck fixed before I had to work on Saturday. My manager at the grocery store let me leave early because business was slow. The NASCAR race wasn't going to start for hours, so I had time to kill. Grandpa was stuck in a traffic jam, and all of my friends were on a field trip. Grandma was at Great-Grandma's place cooking, as she did every Saturday. I decided to drop by the church. I killed the truck and turned my phone off. I sat down in the front row. People were busy getting the church set up for a service later that night. A priest walked by, carrying a round tray filled with ashes. "Here, give me a second."

When he got back, I dove right into it. "So, I know that the Bible says I need to forgive people. I get it as a general principle. It seems like the right thing to do. I only have one problem. If I forgive this guy for what he did to me, then I fear I will be telling him it's okay to do it again. That is not the message I want to send. I am not going through that all over again." The priest took a deep breath. "What are we talking about here?" "It's this guy from school. Actually, it's several people. They have picked on me my whole life. They called me a bunch of names, punched me for no reason, and even told me to kill myself. I overcame that, and I have a good thing going now. If I forgive these people, it could mess everything up. They might take it as me showing weakness or vulnerability. They tend to latch on and attack like vultures. If I don't make them pay, then they could strike again. That's my only reluctance about this whole thing."

He nodded his head. "Is it still happening?" "Well, no. Most of this stuff happened five years ago." He replied, "Then leave it there." I exclaimed, "It's not that simple! You don't know the full story. They are BAD people! I have every right to hate these animals."

He said, "The mouth speaks what the heart is full of. If your spirit is bitter, your words will follow it. Rage is like a wildfire; it's all contained and harmless until it gets too big to control. Your entire life will become engulfed in that anger if you're not careful. You do have the right to let your hatred for them drag you down. It could make you miss out on the life that God wants you to have. Is that what you really want, though?"

I was stumped. I had never thought about it like that. I had no answer. He paused and smiled. "You know what I think? There are several people that you could have talked to, but you chose to come here. Deep down, you probably knew what I was going to say. Before you walked through that door, you knew what you wanted to hear. The decision had already been made. I think you know what you need to do. God won't ask you to give an account of what they did; he will ask about what *you* did. Try not to think about it as having the right to hold a grudge. Imagine having the freedom *not* to. You will experience true freedom after you forgive them. It is the kind of freedom that Christ wants us all to experience, really. If you show them grace, they just might surprise you. I think they will react very differently than you expect them to."

I saw one of the old bullies the following week. I hated this particular guy more than most. This was the same one who claimed to be on my side, then turned on me just a year later. I almost didn't stop, but I knew I needed to. I crossed my arms and looked up. I thought to myself, "All right, fine!" I took a deep breath and turned around. My fists clenched with rage, but I put them in my jacket pocket to hide them. "I've decided to forgive you for what you did. I've hated your guts for a long time, and it's just not worth it anymore. This doesn't make that crap you pulled okay because it wasn't! It never will be. I've just had enough. I'm completely done using my energy to hate you. I hope you deal with whatever hurt you're trying to block out."

I started to walk off when I heard him respond. "There's one thing I never understood about you." I stopped and turned back around. "When people picked on you, why did you put up with it for so long? You used to be a popular kid; what happened?" "Well, I didn't have a choice. I didn't ask to be born with autism!" He paused for a second to gather his thoughts. "Wait, you're autistic?" "Yeah. I can't help that I'm different from most people. I have very little control over that. I had no choice but to put up with it." He slouched his shoulders and replied, "If I knew that, I might have acted differently. You should really tell people that more often."

A few weeks went by, and I finally had the courage to talk to Braxton. I caught him alone in the hallway. A small part of me saw a perfectly good opportunity to smack him with my textbooks. I thought about it for a second but repressed it with my better judgment. "What were you wanting to say to me the other day?" He cleared his throat and looked around to make sure nobody would hear him. He anxiously looked down and avoided eye contact. He finally spoke up. "There is a lot of abuse in my family, and we were going through a divorce back when I picked on you. Several messed-up things have gone on." I rolled my eyes and said, "That is honestly one of the best excuses I've heard yet. I'll give you that." He crunched a piece of paper to suppress his frustration. "What I want to know is how you do it. How are you so happy despite people talking to you the way that they do? I don't get how you're confident in this environment."

I shrugged my shoulders and said, "Well, it's not about me or what people around me say, for that matter. The way I see it, I don't need affirmation from them all the time. Sure, it's a great thing, but it isn't an absolute necessity. I can live a simple life with three or four friends. That's why I have that peace of mind. I don't know where you've been for the last five years, but around here, it honestly isn't that bad anymore. There are still good people out there. I know there are because they are some of my closest friends. The culture here is nothing like that middle school was. People like me all over this building have made bullying a thing of the past. It's just not something we do here; people are willing to speak up when something isn't right. People have changed, and that is part of what changed me. I hope that answers your question." He didn't have any more to say, so we both assumed it was a done deal. He started to pick up his bag.

Before he got away, I said, "For what it's worth, I really hope you get the help you need. I'm not being facetious; I really mean that. Just because you have witnessed abuse doesn't make it normal. It doesn't have to continue being *your* normal either. If you're not happy with your life, there are good therapists out there. I can tell you the name of a psychologist I used to see." A small group walked by us. When he noticed them, he respectfully declined my offer and left.

The priest had certainly been proven right about one thing: Braxton did not react the way I expected he would, not at all. He didn't try to attack me verbally or get violent. He didn't go after my friends as an act of retaliation. He was never aggressive toward me again. I learned that a lot of my fears about him were unfounded. That terror was rooted in a version of him that no longer existed. He wasn't the same guy he was in middle school, and neither was I.

This was long overdue. I had been suppressing this rage for years. Most of the other bullies never apologized. They also never admitted to being in the wrong. They were the toughest ones to forgive, but I eventually did. It took time to let go of the past hurts, even after forgiving them.

When I was finally able to let go of the resentment in my heart, a weight was lifted from my shoulders. I was finally free from everything that happened to me. The past no longer dominated my thoughts. It had no power over me. My peers were not so scary anymore. I stopped being fearful of saying the wrong thing. Autism was no longer an asterisk next to my name. Several of my peers were surprised when I told them I was on the spectrum. It didn't seem as obvious as it once was.

Senior year was great all the way around. My art career went crazy, and my social life started picking up steam. Best of all, this time, I didn't have to put on an act to get it. It was much less work and, quite frankly, more fulfilling. According to social convention, I should've been sad that high school was ending. Truth be told,

I wasn't. I had been going to school with these same people for twelve long years. I knew what it was like to be on their good side, their bad side, and everything in between. I had gone from being treated like a celebrity to being a nobody. I had nothing left to accomplish or prove to them; twelve years was enough.

I pulled up at a diner before the commencement ceremony. There was a long row of pickup trucks in the parking lot. All of my friends were sitting on their tailgates. I glanced over at the old middle school campus. We all knew each other when that school was our battleground. That battle nearly cost me my life, but that wasn't how it was meant to end. My suicidal desires never came back after eighth grade. I never felt that empty numbness inside of me again, not once. It seemed like that was an entire lifetime ago. My mind worked completely differently now than it did back then. Bullying had become a distant memory, one I seldom thought about. The clock seemed to move backward. I experienced the same carefree bliss that I had before the diagnosis. The gap between me and the outside world was smaller than it had ever been. For a long time, I didn't think this day would ever come.

When I walked into the arena for graduation, I wasn't the big star of the bunch. I was finally okay with that. Losing my popularity was the greatest thing that could've happened to me. If I still had an extravagant social life, I wouldn't have invested the time to develop my talents. I also wouldn't have humbled myself for my own good. I found that true freedom wasn't the absence of rules. It was choosing to follow the right rules, the ones that I could live with. Despite what I was told, bad people were not always the winners in life. There was hope for someone like me; I had plenty to show for it in the end. The path to get here was found in God and choosing friends who were good influences on me.

The company I kept had a bigger impact than I thought. Choosing the right relationships led to victory over bullying. It all started when I quit putting my hope in popularity and status; neither was sustainable. Both came crashing down, so I turned to a steadier foundation. I thought I knew what happiness was before that, but I didn't. My new source of confidence could no longer be shaken. My life felt fuller than ever before. That was true freedom: the kind that I had always wanted.

I became living proof that autism did not have to define a person. The bullies did not get the final say in my life; I did.

Epilogue

Autism would eventually prove to be a blessing. I was eligible for scholarships and financial aid that covered all room and board expenses. All I needed to do was show up and do the work. I didn't waste any time getting started.

I was accepted to study graphic design. On the first day, the instructor told us that this program would be the hardest thing we had ever done. He asserted that half of us would not make it. The class got smaller in a rapid fashion. I definitely understand why this happened. I continued pushing through the barriers, one course at a time. I put in many late nights and never let myself quit. Eventually, all of that paid off.

My instructors began to recognize my artistic talent. They emphasized how my skill progression would help me achieve my dreams. They encouraged me to go out and promote my work. I ended up freelancing with countless racecar drivers and teams. I sold prints and took my art business to new heights. I traveled a lot and made connections that were valuable for my career. I also interviewed with some of my dream companies. After two years of the grind, I graduated with academic honors. I needed to transfer to a college that offered a bachelor's degree in my field. I chose one of the largest Christian universities in the country.

I moved back home for my online bachelor's degree. As I unpacked the boxes from my dorm room, I saw something in a drawer. It was a blue wristband with faded ink. I knew where it came from. My mind was immediately flooded with memories. I was back in the middle school auditorium looking at a photograph of a boy in a camo jacket. A guy came onto the stage wearing a white tee shirt with blue text. It said, "I stand for the silent." Wearing a camo hat, he carried a huge clump of blue wristbands with the same lettering. He walked up to the microphone, gave it a couple of test taps, and cleared his throat. "My name is Kirk, but more importantly, I'm Ty's dad." The kid in the picture had been bullied to the ultimate limit. He was lost to suicide at eleven years old.

Several kids in Oklahoma City heard about the tragedy. It led them to launch an anti-bullying organization. Ty's father traveled to schools all over the country to speak about this issue. He hoped to ensure this would never happen to another family. This cause was personal for me because the truth is that I came very close to that same fate. If things hadn't worked out exactly as they did, my story could have ended just like Ty's. I was not alone there by any means. We learned that 25 percent of teens have planned how they would take their own lives before graduating high school. We were also told that it is the second leading cause of death in the 10-to-24-year age range. Statistically, someone is bullied every seven seconds.

He paused and asked all of us a question. "How many of you have been bullied recently?" Roughly two-thirds of the room raised their hands. Several of our teachers did as well. "How many of you are brave enough to admit that you have been a bully?" The tension rose, and a bunch of hands went down. Everyone was awkwardly staring. I didn't want to draw attention to myself, so I raised mine slowly. When I did, people saw me. One guy shook his head and smiled back as he put his hand back up. The brave ones followed suit. Ten hands turned into thirty or so. The speaker took a deep breath and said, "I really appreciate y'all's honesty. I need you to be brave one more time. How many of you have ever felt hopeless before? I'm talking about the kind that is deep; you feel like there's no way out. If this has crossed your mind, even for a split second, please raise your hand. I promise not to interrogate you. I just want the truth." One hand rose in the front row, and others slowly followed. I hesitantly raised mine. When I did, several eyebrows raised. Everyone was shocked by what they were seeing. The speaker got slightly choked up. He looked around and said, "That is a lot of hands. Much more than I expected! This is a real thing, guys. Look around you. Are you seeing the same thing that I do?" He paused to let the students look at all the hands up. He reminded us that it's not always obvious. Many people assumed they knew when a person was depressed. They thought they could tell by the look on someone's face or a sad demeanor. The truth was much more shocking; several hands were up that nobody expected to see. He used this shocking discovery to tell us how dangerous bullying really was. At the end of the presentation, he helped us realize the power we had in our grasp. He made a peace gesture and said, "We can stop this! It doesn't have to be this way. You. Are. Somebody!" He started tossing wristbands out into the crowd that said "I Am Somebody" on them. I caught one and put it on. Several of the popular kids were doing it too.

I got fired up because those numbers were absolutely unacceptable. Schools had finally started making strides to stop this. Unfortunately, there was only so much that they could do. The administration could not fully stop bullying; only we could. I promised myself that I would do something about it when I got older. Over the years, the ink on the wristband faded out. I tossed it in a drawer and left it there. When bullying was no longer a part of my daily life, I slowly lost the fire for it. After I rediscovered the wristband, I decided that it was time for me to support the anti-bullying campaign again. I bought a new one and started wearing it everywhere, just like I used to. Perhaps seeing it would spark a conversation with a person in need of encouragement.

I became a substitute teacher, and the fire was reignited even more. I couldn't wait ten or twenty years to do something to help those people. The stakes were too high. I felt a calling hit my heart to tell this part of my story to people. When it did, I knew that I needed to follow orders. I hooked up my laptop and started typing. I found my old CD collection and listened to it to jog my memory. I then went online and rediscovered the popular music from my middle school era. Suddenly, it all came rushing back. I was reliving those timeframes of my life. I remembered it all as though it were yesterday. Even though the pain was part of the memory, it had to be told honestly; the journey was necessary.

It took me several years to start talking about what really happened to me. Grandma already knew about most of the past but telling Grandpa was on me. I eased into it by asking questions about what God's voice sounded like and how to recognize it. He asked me where this was coming from. I finally opened up about my past experience. He was clearly taken aback. He quit sipping his tea and set it down. He nodded his head. "Y...yep, that's about what it sounds like, all right." He smiled and jokingly said, "It would appear that you have been...chosen!" I freaked out and exclaimed, "Can you please keep your mouth shut about this? I don't want people thinking I'm a crazy religious fanatic. They wouldn't believe it really happened anyway." I nervously bit my lip and looked around to ensure that nobody was eavesdropping. He got up to check the ribs on the barbecue grill before putting his hands in his pockets. He smiled and said, "Yeah, but there's no way you will keep it a secret forever." "Well, you, Grandma, and a priest are the only people I have told. Unless one of you blabs about it, it will be." He cleaned his glasses off and lit the next cigarette. "Oh no, we aren't the ones who will be telling it. You are. When God does something like that, it is usually bigger than just you. He knows how to use stories like that. He's going to have you do something with it. You watch and see." I rolled my eyes and mumbled, "I am not going to tell a bunch of random people I don't know about this! I am not qualified to do that kind of stuff." The fact that you are reading this only proves Grandpa's point. This story is not really about me.

My battles with bullying were not the hardest part for me to write about. Even my near-death experience fails by comparison. The toughest thing was telling the stupid mistakes I made for the sake of popularity. I still roll my eyes with disgust when I see pictures from seventh grade. They represent a chapter of my life that I am not proud of. I remember nearly everything, even the embarrassing details I wish I could forget. Grandma and I debated about whether we should take those pictures off our wall. She won that argument, which means they kept hanging. My hope is that you won't have to make those same mistakes to know what I do. At first, I was concerned that my checkered past would undermine this book's message. I imagined the critics saying, "This guy is not qualified to talk about bullying. He's done it himself!" As I wrote this book, I realized that my past made me more qualified to speak about bullying, not less. I had experienced both sides. I saw a bigger picture than most people, who have only been on one side. I formed a deep understanding of what goes through the mind of a bully. I also knew what it was like on the other side.

People complain that kids these days are becoming more brutal and mean than ever before. Some blame the parents, some blame the schools, while others blame those "darned video games." They claim that today's kids have no respect for anybody and that there are no good ones left. Based on my experience, I don't see much truth behind that. There are many people just like me out there who do care about others. Most of them want to see bullying come to an end. They just don't know where to start. Many of them doubt it is even possible.

The negative voices are often the ones that get heard first because they are the loudest. We need to be just as bold as they are to make things happen. Changing a school culture requires a great deal of work; it takes more than one person. However, it takes only one conversation to start that train. If a person is willing to call out a bully, others may follow in their footsteps. One person can inspire hundreds of bystanders to stand up for what is right. One of the most underrated Bible verses is Proverbs 18:21. It tells us that we have the power of life and death in our tongues.

I hope my story inspires you to "Stand for The Silent" and help end bullying. Give the new kid at your school a chance. That autistic kid in the corner is not the freaky creature they seem to be. People like me share many of the same fears and desires that you have. Some of the coolest people you'll ever know are sitting in the back of a classroom drawing or playing with Legos right now.

Take a stand. Change a life. You have a reason.

Acknowledgments

My grandparents deserve a ton of credit for raising an autistic child. I know it was not easy. They freely chose to raise me and gave me their constant love and support. They made many sacrifices to give me a good life. Not every autistic person has the support system that I was blessed to have. I am constantly reminded of how good I really had it. My grandparents had the help of speech therapists, psychologists, and far too many good teachers to mention. My family is certainly too large to name them all.

Thanks to my lifelong friends, especially Andrew. I know I wasn't always easy to deal with. I failed all of you on many occasions. At one point, I was disloyal and even unbearable. You taught me what compassion and forgiveness were all about. I could never fully repay my debt to you. I did the best I could to include all of our memories in this book. Unfortunately, I could not squeeze my whole life story into one project. If I wrote everything, people would have gray hair before they finished this book! You guys know that better than I do. I am lucky to still be able to call you all my friends.

I have been fortunate enough to date beautiful women in my life. To every girl who had an influence on me, thanks. Charlotte, thank you for those two years of support. They pushed me to become assertive enough to stand up to bullying. Life is good. That's the way it should be: bright.

I appreciate everyone who took time out of their busy lives to be interviewed. I have a good memory, but it's not perfect. I needed help getting the details right. That is where your stories came into play. The interviews taught me things about myself that I didn't even know. Each one played a role in shaping the final product. My name may be listed as the author, but the interviewees did a lot of the heavy lifting behind the scenes.

To Kirk Smalley and Stand for the Silent®, thanks for all you're doing to end bullying. Your efforts are not in vain. Those blue "I Am Somebody" wristbands were more than a slogan for my peers and me. They contributed to real change in our school culture. I watched this anti-bullying organization touch countless lives. SFTS was a big part of my inspiration to produce this book. The memory of Ty Smalley and every kid lost to suicide should not be forgotten. This organization needs the help of supporters like you and me to continue fighting this tragic cycle. You can empower youth to stand above bullying at StandForTheSilent.org.

Did you enjoy this book? It will mean the world to me
if you write a review or share on social media!

You can connect with me at JoeyPerryArts.com
or @JoeyPerryArts on most platforms.

CPSIA information can be obtained
at www.ICGtesting.com
Printed in the USA
JSHW020702271122
33692JS00009B/20